Pioneer Life
In Western Pennsylvania

BY J. E. WRIGHT

AND DORIS S. CORBETT

Pioneer Life

ILLUSTRATIONS BY CLARENCE McWILLIAMS

In Western
Pennsylvania

UNIVERSITY OF PITTSBURGH PRESS

THE AUTHORS *gratefully acknowledge their in-debtedness to the Masters thesis of Mary Sterrett Moses, "Pioneer Women in Western Pennsylvania," for some of the ideas contained in Chapter IX.*

THIS BOOK *is one of a series relating West-*
ern Pennsylvania history, written under the
direction of the Western Pennsylvania His-
torical Survey sponsored jointly by The Buhl
Foundation, the Historical Society of Western
Pennsylvania and the University of Pittsburgh.

CONTENTS

I	The Way of the Frontier	1
II	First Footprints	12
III	How the Settler Got His Land	26
IV	The Cabin in the Clearing	41
V	Linsey and Buckskin: Venison and Pone	54
VI	Truck Patch and Cornfield	64
VII	Butcher, Baker, Candlestick-Maker	74
VIII	Growing Up on the Frontier	84
IX	Jigging It Off	101
X	"Indians in the Valley!"	117
XI	Yarbs, Doctors, and Charms	129
XII	The Log Church	140
XIII	Frontier Justice	158
XIV	From Indian Trail to Turnpike	175
XV	Life in the Towns	200
XVI	The First Factories	220
XVII	The Road to the Past	232
	Glossary	243

Pioneer Life
In Western Pennsylvania

The Way of the Frontier

I

FROM a sky as blue as the chicory in the grass, sunlight fell across a clearing and reached golden fingers back among the trees. The clearing itself, its leaf-molded surface, was marked with fresh-cut stumps and littered with yellow flakes and chips that the ax had cut from the trunks piled roughly to one side—trunks not yet trimmed of their branches and freshly pointed from the blows of the ax.

On one of the stumps in the clearing sat a man and his wife. The sleeve of his linsey hunting shirt was ripped, his brown leggings were half hidden by the blue folds of her full, rough skirt, and his feet in their scuffed shoepacks braced the ground for support as if he was ready to spring erect at a sound. His hunting shirt, held close about his waist by a belt and lapping over double in front, hung with its red fringe almost to his knees. At his elbow stood his rifle. His other hand steadied the ax, and from the polished edge of its blade the sun struck light.

Such figures were part of the everyday picture of pioneer life in western Pennsylvania. The settler and the woman who made his cabin a home must often have paused, in many a clearing in the forests that covered the western end of the state, to look for a moment at what they had done. The long road they had recently left led west no longer. They had reached its end. It ran east now, from the clearing on the frontier's edge. These were moments when, tired but hopeful, they stopped to realize not the struggle but the beauty, not the doubts but the achievements, not the weariness and hardship of the journey but the rest and the promise of home. Now they could look, not at thickset trees to be cut and the unfinished door or chimney of their cabin, not at the rough-surfaced ground to be plowed and the threat of storm in the sky, but at the sunlight in the clearing as it fell on the scattered tree chips and the chicory flowers at their feet, when the hand could be free of the rifle and could relax on the haft of the ax.

These were the true pioneers, the man and woman who had come out on foot, driving perhaps one lean cow or carrying all their belongings on their backs. During the first year of their life in the wilderness they ate mostly potatoes and slept on clean leaves gathered in the woods. These first settlers found seed so scarce that when a hen ate the melon seeds laid in the sun to dry they cut open the hen's crop and sewed it up again, so as not to lose either the seeds or the hen. They were the kind of men and women who would rather live in crude cabins set in small and slovenly clearings than remain as indentured servants in the eastern counties and states; the kind of men and women who worked on, half-starved for lack of proper food because they had been tricked by land speculators into thinking they were going into a land of honey and milk; the kind of men and women who had accepted the hard life of the frontier because land in the East was scarce and expensive. These were the early home-makers who, because they often could not afford oxen or horses to draw their plows, were unable to cultivate their lands properly and could only scratch over the surface with a dead branch or at best a hoe. But they were the people who had the courage to face hardship and death, who had great physical strength, who were impatient of discipline, and who were capable of fighting for their own beliefs.

Ahead lay endless trouble—sheep and hogs devoured by wolves; horses and cattle wandering into the fields and trampling the growing grain; corn destroyed by squirrels and raccoons; crops ruined by frost or drought. The men worked in the fields with their rifles, those who could afford them, stacked close by under the watch of a sentinel. The women were the pioneer mothers who came to the frontier young, healthy, and strong-hearted, who undertook endless household duties, who endured loneliness, starvation, dread of Indian massacre, and perhaps the grief of seeing their children and husbands taken into captivity. These men and women the frontier took, drained from them the strength and freshness of youth, and left them creased and browned and warped, old men and women at thirty-five.

CHURNING BUTTER

These people, with ax and maul and wedge, had set out to wrest from this new life the economic security denied them in the place whence they had come. With no other tools, frequently, but with grim, set purpose, they were determined to win self and community respect. And often they attained real happiness.

The real pioneer was a home-maker, a cabin builder. He had come West for many reasons, but first among them always was the desire to get land, raise his cabin, and win a living for himself and his family in his own way. In the wilderness homes along the streams and roads and on the hills of western Pennsylvania was born that free spirit which marks the laws and institutions of our present-day civilization. The home-making pioneer, in organizing his family life, organized the life of his community. In erecting his cabin in the clearing, he erected the symbol of America for years to come.

The pioneer was hard-featured. Lean and weather-beaten, often stooped by hardship and toil, his skin an unhealthy color from improper food, he was not always the hearty, robust man one would expect from active life in the open. Border life was particularly harsh with women. The dates on old gravestones show that many died years before their husbands, and often several women bore the same man's name. Widows were few; they remarried for protection and to guard against starving. Many children died at birth or in their first year or two of life. If they grew to manhood or womanhood they became the typical, sinewy, roughened frontiersmen and frontier mothers. Poor sanitation and lack of hygienic knowledge bred skin diseases and lice. Cleanliness was difficult, and illiteracy common. But there is a great deal more to the story than that, as we shall see.

The pioneer was industrious. Only hard work day after day built his log cabin, made his puncheon floors, his split-log bed frames and tables. Only strenuous digging, sowing, raking, and threshing would provide his family with grain and vegetables. There was hunting to be done, for game which he hauled home to skin, cut up, and cure.

CRADLE

The pioneer was resourceful. He had to be, with few tools, without shops and stores to run to for his wants, and with few near neighbors to give advice and help. He had harsh weather and wild beasts to contend with. When ill or the victim of an accident in the woods or along the trails he had no first-aid kit of handy remedies. He faced danger from the Indians. And he had at times to deal with wrong-thinking, wrong-doing men— a thief, a land cheat, or a deliberate squatter. All these problems had to be dealt with quickly; otherwise, he lost out. He might lose property, the few furnishings of his home, or even his life. He might lose his health or his reputation as an honest man. Against such things he had to be constantly on guard.

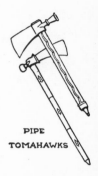

PIPE
TOMAHAWKS

Bravery in Indian raids and battles had to be joined with courage to bear pain—a wound from an accidental discharge of a gun, a gash from a knife or an ax, a snake bite, an arm or leg muscle torn in a hidden trap or in a fight with a bear.

The frontier demanded far more than physical courage. Lonely months had to be endured, in which no stranger or friend passed by the little cabin. Family ties, broken when settlers started out for the new lands, pulled at the heartstrings. News came from the old, far-away world of the death of a brother or a sister. Worry about food when stores ran low in winter, suffering from disease when no doctor or remedy was at hand, and times of longing for the old life with its brighter, more comfortable days often discouraged the pioneer. There were men and women, broken in health and spirit, whose minds were not strong enough to fight against worry and despair brought on by loneliness or by Indian captivity and possible torture of members of their families. Early records contain many stories of strange people living alone—hermits, witches, and other queer characters that life had bent out of their natural shapes. All these things were the price the pioneers paid to win a new world for later generations. But greater than their sufferings were their hope and their faith in the life they had chosen.

One of these early settlers has left a description of the first years of his life with his family on the edge of the frontier:

"It was very lonesome for several years. People would move in, and stay a short time, and move away again. . . . I started, with my two yoke of oxen, to go to Jersey Shore, to mill, to procure flour. I crossed Pine Creek eighty times going to, and eighty times coming from mill, was gone eighteen days, broke two axletrees to my wagon, upset twice, and one wheel came off in crossing the creek. . . .

"The few seeds that I was able to plant the first year, yielded but little produce. We however raised some half-grown potatoes, some turnips, and soft corn, with which we made out to live, without suffering, till the next spring, at planting time, when I planted all the seeds that I had left; and when I finished planting, we had nothing to eat but leeks, cow-cabbage, and milk. We lived on leeks and cow-cabbage as long as they kept green—about six weeks. . . . during the three winter months it snowed 70 days. I sold one yoke of my oxen in the fall, the other yoke I wintered on browse; but in the spring one ox died, and the other I sold to procure food for my family, and was now destitute of a team, and had nothing but my own hands to depend upon to clear my lands and raise provisions. We wore out all our shoes the first year. We had no way to get more,—

no money, nothing to sell, and but little to eat,—and were in dreadful distress for the want of the necessaries of life. I was obliged to work and travel in the woods barefooted. After a while our clothes were worn out. Our family increased, and the children were nearly naked. I had a broken slate that I brought from Jersey Shore. I sold that . . . and bought two fawn-skins, of which my wife made a petticoat for Mary; and Mary wore the petticoat until she outgrew it; then Rhoda took it till she outgrew it; then Susan had it, till she outgrew it; then it fell to Abigail, and she wore it out."

How true this picture is we know from comparing it with other records of the early years when the wilderness of western Pennsylvania was being prepared for the farms and well-built towns that we pass now while driving over smooth roads that often follow the early trails made by these pioneer men and women.

And yet because of his solitude the pioneer was hospitable, hailing and welcoming the stranger to his home. One of those pleasant books that contain first-hand accounts of pioneer life, John L. McConnel's *Western Characters or Types of Border Life in the Western States,* relates how the stranger was received in the frontier cabin:

"But he [*the pioneer*] is neither unsocial, nor morose. He welcomes the stranger as heartily as the most hospitable patriarch. He receives the sojourner at his fireside without question. He regales him with the best the house affords: is always anxious to have him 'stay another day.' He cares for his horse, renews his harness, laughs at his stories, and exchanges romances with him. He hunts with him; fishes, rides, walks, talks,

DUTCH OVEN

eats, and drinks with him. His wife washes and mends the stranger's shirts, and lends him a needle and thread to sew a button on his only pair of pantaloons. The children sit on his knee, the dog lies at his feet, and accompanies him into the woods. The whole family are his friends, and only grow cold and distant when they learn that he is looking for land, and thinks of 'settling' within a few leagues. If nothing of the sort occurs—and this only 'leaks out' by accident, for the pioneer never pries inquisitively into the business of his guest, he keeps him as long as he can; and when he can stay no longer, fills his saddle-bags with flitches of bacon and 'pones' of corn-bread, shakes him heartily by the hand, exacts a promise to stop again on his return, and bids him 'God-speed' on his journey."

The same scarcity of acquaintances and associates that made the pioneer warm and constant in friendship also made him bitterly angry at injustice done to him, to his family, or to his belongings. People who live much alone feel ordinary human emotions the more strongly, perhaps, because the emotions are stored up and when they find expression they pour out more violently for having been pent up so long. If frontier revenge seems sometimes extreme to us, if frontier justice and punishments seem sometimes harsh and cruel, we must take conditions into account.

A historian who has studied very carefully the frontier in American history writes of the decline of knowledge on the frontier and of the increase of "lawlessness," in the sense of the pioneer's disregard of those laws that he considered unnecessary or unjust. We must admit that what he says has truth in it. Books and papers were scarce, and much of what the pio-

FLINTLOCK PISTOLS

neer had learned in his earlier settled community, with its schools, churches, libraries, and papers, became useless and was forgotten. These facts explain the rawness of early American civilization; but they also explain its strength and promise. In many a family's scant belongings, however, carried over the mountains in cart or on pack horse, or on foot in a cloth-wrapped bundle, was a Bible or a copy of Shakespeare. From the Bible more than one frontier child learned to read by fire-light or rushlight. And these little flames of culture and knowl-edge were cared for as carefully as the rows of beans and pump-kins outside the cabin door.

The "lawlessness" of the frontiersman might be explained by his refusal to be wronged, his independence, his courage, his active sense of justice. Lawlessness, in its true sense, means the breaking of just and reasonable laws. This is not characteristic of Americans. Americans have inherited from these pioneer men and women, who had been trained in the hard school of experience to win the rights of "life, liberty, and the pursuit of happiness," an unusual sense of what is just in lawmaking. It was to establish these rights more firmly that pioneers strug-gled in the wilderness; they wanted personal liberty and eco-nomic freedom, the right to a full life. In the pursuit of happi-ness these men and women sought the unsettled lands of the western country. And they defended their enterprise sturdily, whether they were threatened by poor living, Indians, illness and hunger, or by unjust officials and intruders.

Frontier people were often grave and heavy-spirited. Howl-ing winter winds, the cry of wolves, the screech of owls through the clearing—such sounds on the strained ears of a family huddled close to the crude chimney place in a smoke-filled cabin night after night might start their minds working upon fantastic ideas. Such sounds came to be omens of misfortune—of accident, illness, and death. Often enough they were heard when worry had already turned the thoughts of the listeners toward trouble that could be seen ahead. The pioneers thought and felt in ways strange to us, ways not at all practical but highly imaginative, although not properly so. For instance, it takes imagination to associate the baying of a dog with the death of some one you love, but it is not healthy imagination. It takes imagination to feel that the cry of an owl means danger ahead, but that, too, is not healthy imagination. There was, of course, some reason for thinking an owl's cry was a warning, for prowling Indians might have disturbed the bird. But the pioneer made many unreasonable associations between sounds and misfortunes and became a superstitious person.

Yet these people were not always somber and pathetic, not always straining body and mind to earn a bare living. Simple and plain in person, dress, and speech, the pioneer yet broke out occasionally into salty speech and dashing, boisterous action. At house raisings and weddings, at quilting bees and *schnitzens* (apple parings), there was a great deal of rough festivity. In the cramped cabins, on the puncheon floors, lit by the faint radiance of tallow dips or smoky pine knots or by the smelly wicks of Betty lamps, happy groups would dance and swirl, noisily, unrestrainedly, because such occasions were rare. And the faint light brought out the soft color of homespun dresses, red and blue and saffron yellow. The brown breeches and leggings of the men in their checkered hunting shirts wove in and out among twirling skirts to the scratching tune of a fiddle in the corner, in the firelight. Or, on a summer night, the same scene took place outside the cabin, where moonlight slanted across the dancing forms and softened the figures and the crude homespun garments.

So we see the frontiersman as a many-sided personality. This new and difficult life that he faced made him in turn open-natured or reserved; stern or gay; heroic, yet as often pitiable. And he never lost a sense of beauty and wonder. The fury of winds and storms, though threatening and disastrous, held him in awe. He saw day after day the beech trunks gilded by sunlight and the dimness of great forests, quiet as a sleeping child. He saw the violets by the palisades and the wild mint by the creek edge. He saw the sun flame over the mountains and DOGWOOD the purple of twilight deepen to thick black of night. Blue shadows on Christmas snows, the orange sunsets of January, the gurgle of water under thawing ice in February, and the winds that tossed the branches of the pines in March; the first shrill songs of the tree toads in April, the meadows of bluebells in May, the fresh fields of rye and wheat well-sprung in June, and the hot, starry nights in July when the birds had grown silent—all the pageant of the year spread sights and sounds around him. Living always at the heart of nature, he could not fail to feel the beat of that great heart.

First Footprints

I I

O N NO map showing the country before 1700 is the section
that we know today as western Pennsylvania definitely
outlined. This country around the headwaters of the Ohio
River, then called the Ohio or the western country, was to
the white man an unlimited and unexplored region. When
the forerunners of settlement first came through the gaps in
the Allegheny Mountains made by the Juniata River and
descended the last slope of Laurel Hill, they knew they had
passed beyond the western limits of settled country and had
entered the upper Ohio Valley, but just where the western
boundaries of this new region lay they did not know. The
"vast level sea of waving tree tops" stretching from the foot
of the slope reached to Lake Erie in the north and somewhere
about the Potomac River in the south and it was drained by
a system of three main rivers—the Allegheny, the Monongahela, and the Youghiogheny—and their tributaries of lesser
rivers and creeks. Most of the waterways, even in their upper
reaches, were navigable by canoe, and some of them by larger
craft. From the settlements that first sprang up in the Monongahela Valley, or from the north by way of the Allegheny River,

the pioneers later transported themselves and their goods to the forks of the Ohio, from where, although the two streams merged, the greener water of the Allegheny still kept its identity some distance down country.

This uncharted headwater country was covered with many kinds of trees. The commonest large trees were the oak, pine, hemlock, chestnut, and tulip trees. Ash, wild plum, and sycamore trees were also plentiful, and in the southern section there were more chestnut, walnut, and hickory than in the northern part. Seen from the last ridge of the mountains, however, the region appeared only as a "forest of leaves." As trader or hunter descended into the wilderness, he came upon a realm of dense shadows and silence. The thick green gloom was caused largely by an overhead curtain of wild grapevines, which climbed from branch to branch and tangled together the tops of the trees. As he pushed on, deer and elk started at his footstep or gun crack, and bears lumbered out of his path. Wild cats flashed through the brush, and rattlesnakes coiled and sounded their alarm at his progress.

PIGNUT HICKORY

This Ohio or western country offered the oncoming white men what they sought. It offered them opportunity, freedom, and the "elbowroom" that so many pioneers felt they must have. There land was to be had almost for the taking. And with the land they would get what they needed to keep alive, if they were willing to face hard work and to do without many comforts. There were furs for the trader, game for the hunter, lumber for cabins and fires, and fruits and nuts for the settler until his vegetable patch yielded a crop, however small, and the forests were thought to mean fertile soil, which, when cleared,

would grow his grain. Later, with the advancement of settlement, the streams would turn the wheels of his mill and the
ground would furnish coal, sandstone, and limestone, and clay
for brick-making. This new western country, which was first
visited by Indian traders and hunters, held everything to help
civilization grow from its first stages of agricultural settlement, through the crude beginnings of industrial activity, to
a great network of cities and towns.

But except for a visit in 1691 by the Albany trader, Arnold
Viele, the Ohio country was unknown to white men until
1720. The only smoke that rose in its forests, against its
skies, came from the campfires of the Iroquois, whose hunting
ground it was. The only craft on its streams were their bark
and log canoes. The only paths were their narrow, winding
trails.

Then about 1720 the Shawnee, whose hunting grounds had
been in eastern and central Pennsylvania, were pushed westward by the growth of agricultural settlement there into this
wilderness country. Close on their heels followed the traders
and trappers, eager for pelts and furs. Hunters' rifles, bringing
down the elk and the deer, began to crack in the forests. Smoke
from the traders' campfires began to drift over the western
waters. But for thirty years after these first adventurers came
into the section no settler's cabin hung out its latch-string of
deer thong and burned its smoking pine knots in the night.

Before the western wilderness could be cleared and land
broken for farms, before the frontiersman and his wife could
settle into their business of home-making, much preparation
was needed. It was the mission of the Indian trader to do much

PACKHORSE   TRAIN

of this preparation, to be the forerunner of the true pioneer, who was the home-maker and farmer. It was the trader who widened the first trails with his pack horse. He first followed the streams, charting their courses and the lay of the hills, marking on his crude maps the locations of the Indian towns and trading posts. He noted the trees and shrubs, the kinds of game in the forests, and the fish in the streams. He saw where coal lay near the surface, where clay could be used for bricks, and where salt springs could be found. He learned the advantages of Indian dress and the ways of Indian warfare and advised the settlers who followed. He learned what berries, bark, and plants could be eaten and which could be used for cures.

The trader was often a diplomat, dealing with Indian tribes, winning their friendship, organizing their trade, or treating with them for lands.

He was sometimes a boatman, going up and down the rivers which, taken together, were called the western waters, exploring new creeks in bark or dugout canoe, and reaching the most distant spots to establish his trading posts. But generally he was a pack-horse man. His goods were brought over the mountains on the backs of wiry ponies, and since he more often forded the rivers than followed them it was more practical to continue toward the west with pack horses than by boat. The French traders who brought their goods from Montreal, since they followed the water route most of the way, naturally used boats.

At times the trader served as a scout, not attached to any particular fort or company and not a professional soldier, but appointed and sent out at need as a guide, a messenger, or a spy. George Croghan, the famous trader, wrote to General

Braddock that these men should be enlisted to dress, march, and fight as they pleased, without being subject to the strict regulations of a soldiers' camp.

Too often the Indian trader was just a plain rascal, roaming the country as a freebooter, cheating, lying, and bartering rum with the Indians, murdering if it suited his purposes, burning out Indians or white men—unclean, unjust, immoral. Sir William Johnson in 1767 characterized them as "the very dregs of the people," and from them, he said, "regularity, honesty, or discretion could not be expected."

Yet there were many fine men among them. One of these, named James Kenny, was for some time between the years 1759 and 1763 employed in the trading store established by the province of Pennsylvania at Pittsburgh. He was a Quaker and represented the best type among the traders. Kenny kept a journal that tells from day to day of his affairs on the frontier. With its quaint spelling, abbreviations, and punctuation it makes delightful reading.

"One of ye Mingo Warriors," he writes, "brot a Beaver late in ye Evening, it came to 2½ lb Powder, so I took his Bag & went for ye Powdr by myself, he scruppled my measure, I told him there was 2½ Pints but he wanted to see it measur'd, so I measured it & it held out Large measure; I laugh'd at him & he Clapt me on ye Shoulder & sd it was right." Kenny gives us some idea of the amount of trade carried on: "Jack Stroud, & 3 Waggons more came here, he brot sundry Goods." Or he writes, "Load'd two Waggons with Peltry yesterday and they set off; I sent my Wolf, Racoon & Wild Cat, a present to ye Governor." Kenny also tells how attempts were made to regulate the Indian trade. "There is a Proclamation from Collo¹ Johnson Posted up here for all yᵉ Indian Traders to Adhere to, yᵉ Prices of yᵉ Goods that is now fix'd at a more benefishal profit than here before; all yᵉ Traders to have a Pass from Sʳ Wᵐ Johnson or George Croughan Esqʳ else yᵉ Commanding officiers at each Post are forbid to let them Trade."

Many of the traders became famous for qualities that made life on the frontier easier than it might have been without their services. The career of one of them, James O'Hara, demonstrates the changes through which early settlement passed. O'Hara was first of all, in 1773, an Indian trader. He became a government agent among the Indians, a diplomat to encourage friendship. In the Revolutionary War he was captain of a volunteer company. He was appointed quartermaster-general of the United States Army in 1792, and he served during General Wayne's expedition against the Indians. He represented the first stages in the growth of industry when he formed a partnership with Major Isaac Craig for the manufacture of glass in Pittsburgh. He built ocean vessels for the Liverpool trade and aided as well in the development of river traffic. He had a part in the growth of business through the period when banking became necessary, for he was president, then director, of the Pittsburgh branch of the Bank of Pennsylvania. He took part in the first stages of the most important industry of western Pennsylvania, for he was a partner in certain ironworks at Ligonier. He was also interested in the real estate business in the rapidly growing town of Pittsburgh. By that time the pioneer age in western Pennsylvania had passed; a settled civilization had come to stay.

POWDER KEG

Other men who engaged in Indian trading were George Croghan, said to have been "worth more than a garrison in troublous times," Richard Butler, and George Morgan—all of whom built up great fortunes for their day. John Gibson was a trader, an Indian captive, a commander in the Revolution, and secretary of the Indiana Territory. Alexander Lowrey and Alexander Maginty did valuable work for Lewis Evans in making his maps of the new lands.

The professional trader obtained his skins and furs from the Indians and from those white men who searched the woods with rifles to bring down the wild animals whose skins served as money in the purchase of the goods they needed from the East. The hunter, in his half Indian dress, the color of the brown leaves of autumn, made his way mile upon mile through virgin forest; he wore a hunting shirt of doeskin or linsey, breeches of the same materials, moccasins or shoepacks, a coonskin cap on his head, over one shoulder on a leather thong his powder horn, at his belt a tomahawk and a leather bullet bag with squirrel tail hanging for ornament. He carried his provisions on his back, or in the full front of his shirt he stuffed tow and flint for fire, a piece of dried venison or jerk, and a small bag of meal to be made into hard cake on a stone by his campfire. At night he had only a tree for shelter, or a half-faced Indian camp if he took time to erect it. He tracked the woods with eyes alert for every sight of antlers and every scurrying squirrel, for every change of sky that promised change of weather, for every variation in the way smoke rose and drifted; with ears tuned for every snapping twig and scuffle of leaves, for every animal call or cry as clues to locating game.

He guided himself by the signs of nature—the moss on tree trunks, the direction and length of shadows, the courses of streams, the positions of particular trees or stones. He was geographer, botanist, astronomer, geologist; he was his own butcher, his own cook, his own doctor in case of accident. He knew the properties of plant and herb and the habits of bird and beast. All this lore he used to stalk deer, to trap bear, to shoot fox and raccoon.

When the leaves had fallen and the first thin snow lay over them, then the long hunt took place. Fall and early winter were the seasons for hunting deer, the whole of winter and part of spring for fur-bearing animals. The long hunter, sometimes with a hunting dog and a horse to carry provisions, set out for the spot where he knew he would erect his half-faced camp, on some site protected by hills from the north and west winds. A single large log served as the back of his shelter. Eight or ten feet in front stakes were driven into the ground to receive the upper ends of the roof poles. The roof sloped from front to back and was made of slabs, skins, or blankets, or of hickory or ash bark in the spring. The front stood open, and a fire was built directly before it. Moss was stuffed in the cracks; dry leaves served for a bed. Such a three-sided structure was thrown up in a few hours and it protected the hunter from storms. But it was not a protection from Indians; hunters were often surprised and murdered in their camps.

With wonderful skill the long hunter laid his campaign and calculated his chances. If the day was stormy he hunted deer on the leeward side of the hills, where they sought shelter. If the day brought rain but little wind he went to the open woods on

FRONTIERSMAN

high ground. In the morning he moistened his finger in his mouth, then raised it high above his head to see which side dried first. From that side came the wind, which he must learn in order to keep to the leeward of the game. He maneuvered all day to approach his game without discovery, skinned the animals as he found them, and hung the pelts out of reach of the wolves, to be picked up on his return to camp.

Arrived at evening with his catch, he built his fire, cooked his venison and johnnycake, and, if he had a companion, told of the day's long doings, tales of the spike buck, the two and three-pronged buck, and the doe. Then he stretched himself on his bed of leaves and dreamed of the buck with silver horns and the doe that sped on wings.

On the frontier the gun came before the ax or the plow. Men were often hunters before they became settled home-makers. And, more important, armed conflict had to determine the ownership of the region before homes and industries could safely be established. After the traders had told the world about the Ohio country as a place for settlement, the French, the English, and the Indians all claimed it. Baron de Longueuil and his lieutenant, De Léry, led a French expedition from Canada through western Pennsylvania in 1739. In 1747 the Ohio Company was formed by some Virginia gentlemen to extend the settlement of their province into lands around the upper Ohio River claimed under its charter. In 1749 Céloron de Blainville, accompanied by De Léry, led another expedition down the Allegheny and Ohio rivers and claimed them for the French with the lands the two rivers drained. But the following year the Ohio Company sent Christopher Gist to explore the same country so that they might encourage settlers to go there.

The question as to whether the French or the Virginians had the better right to the country was bitterly disputed and soon led to what historians call the French and Indian War. Governor Dinwiddie of Virginia sent George Washington to Fort Le Bœuf (Waterford, Erie County) with a message ordering the French to leave—of course they refused. Captain Trent, upon the orders of Governor Dinwiddie, began to erect a fort at the junction of the Allegheny and Ohio rivers. But before it could be completed it was captured by the French and a new fort, named Fort Duquesne, was erected on the spot. Washington set out in 1754 to take back the fort but was defeated at Great Meadows. General Braddock was sent from England the following year to aid the colonists, but he, too, was defeated not far from the fort. The war between the French and English then became general; the war zone extended from the mouth of the St. Lawrence River to the backwoods of Virginia. Finally in 1758 William Pitt, England's new prime minister, sent General Forbes to command the British troops in Pennsylvania. From Raystown, now Bedford, the edge of western settlement at the time, General Forbes sent Major James Grant with a scouting party to Fort Duquesne. Grant got into a battle with the garrison of the fort and was defeated on the hill overlooking the Point in Pittsburgh that has ever since been known as Grant's Hill. But Forbes in the meantime had advanced from Raystown, the French set fire to the fort and fled. Near its half-burned remains the English erected Fort Pitt.

These events had brought into the frontier new people who shared in paving the way for the settlers to come. For a time soldiers were far more numerous than traders. They commanded scouting parties of redskins, surveyed the mountains and the courses of the rivers, built forts at strategic points, and served as diplomats, making treaties between their governments and the Indians. More than these services in preparing the country for settlement, the soldiers brought new articles to the frontier, among them new plants and seeds to be experimented with in such places as the King's Garden around Fort Pitt. Some of these soldiers were British regulars, and some were Virginia and Pennsylvania militia. After their military service had ended, many of them returned to the western country to take up farms and to found homes.

About the time the first military expeditions came into the region, the missionaries began to enter and to preach Christianity to the Indians. The earliest missionary priests came with the French from Canada and were chiefly Jesuits and Recollect friars. The Jesuits, able, cultured, and enthusiastic, not only took the usual three vows of poverty, chastity, and obedience but also vowed to undertake missionary work in whatever lands to which they might be sent. They traveled the densest forests, followed unknown streams, through bitter winter and withering summer heat, faced hardship, torture, and death to carry Christianity to the Indians and to claim the land. For years after their first appearance it was not uncommon to meet wandering Indians whom they had baptized, Indians with rosaries and crucifixes, who talked of Christianity without understanding.

When, in 1754, Pierre de Contrecœur built Fort Duquesne, his chaplain was Father Denys Baron, whose figure became

familiar in the coarse brown habit of the Recollect friars, with
its cowl and its rope girdle, from which dangled a crucifix.
Father Baron was at Fort Duquesne two years, during which
time he kept a register of births and deaths which has been
preserved. During the four years that the fort was known as
Fort Duquesne other French priests were on duty in the district. The year after Father Baron left, a Jesuit, Father Virot,
planted a mission cross at the mouth of the Big Beaver River.
The same year he was joined by another Jesuit, Father Rou-
boud. When the Ohio country fell to the British, the Wolf
tribe of the local Delaware Indians drove away the French
priests from the Big Beaver, and their share in the history of
the western Pennsylvania frontier was ended.

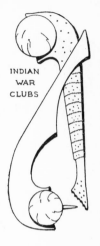

INDIAN
WAR
CLUBS

For fifty years after General Forbes took Fort Duquesne in
the name of the English king, most of the Protestant sects sent
out ministers to both the Indians and the white settlers. With
the Indians they seem to have had little success except for the
work done by the Moravians, Christian Frederick Post, John
Heckewelder, and David Zeisberger.

Post, with two Indian guides, entered the hostile country
just ahead of General Forbes; across the river from Fort Duquesne he held a conference with the Indians that won their
friendship for the English. In 1761, before formal peace was
signed between England and France, he made another journey,
this time as far west as the Tuscarawas River in Ohio. Later
the Moravian brethren at Bethlehem sent him a helper. He was
a young man nineteen years old, John Heckewelder, who, after
many years of service as a missionary, was to write the story of
his work among the Indians.

David Zeisberger in 1767 preached to the Indians in their council house at Goshgoshunk on the left bank of the Allegheny River near the mouth of Tionesta Creek in Venango County. This service must have been a strange sight. The interior of the council house had been arranged as much as possible like a church. In the middle of the floor burned the fire, for warmth. Around it sat the men on one side and the women on the other, wrapped in blankets of red and black, their faces painted, and their bodies decorated with strings of beads. In the midst stood the good Moravian brother, Zeisberger, in simple clerical dress, a close fitting coat without lapels, knee-buckled small clothes, and broad, round-toed shoes. He had laid aside his wide brimmed, shallow hat.

With the help of a new comer of the same sect, Gottlieb Senseman, and three families of Christian Indians, Zeisberger formed another church on the banks of the Allegheny. But in the troublesome times that followed, the church was moved three miles farther north for safety. Zeisberger and Senseman kept in close touch with the young settlement at Pittsburgh. In 1770 the congregation of Indians moved from Goshgoshunk to a site on the Big Beaver River, in Lawrence County, somewhere between the Shenango River and Slippery Rock Creek. The place was called Friedensstadt, or Town of Peace, to distinguish it from the troublesome places that had been abandoned. Zeisberger was joined the next year by John Heckewelder as helper. Zeisberger had so won the admiration of the Indians that they adopted him into their tribe. But the end of Friedensstadt was not a happy one. Drunken Indians from neighboring towns often overran the mission and caused trouble; so Zeisberger concluded that it was best to move the mission farther west to lands already settled by the Moravian Indians along the Tuscarawas River in Ohio.

By their friendly civilizing of these Indians the pioneer Moravian missionaries helped ease the way for settlers in western Pennsylvania. They accompanied the Indians on hunting trips, paddled in their canoes, and fished with them. In this way they learned the Indian language and taught their language to the Indians. In the missions these men taught the Indians to build substantial log houses, and they conducted schools where the beginnings of reading and writing were taught. Each mission had a log chapel. Fields and gardens were laid out and fenced. Hogs, horses, cattle, and poultry were brought from the East. The Indians learned to do simple carpentry and such blacksmithing as they needed.

One of the final steps in opening the Ohio country for settlement was the battle of Bushy Run. Forbes had won from the French the right to English settlement, but the Indians who had joined with the French to fight the English were not satisfied with the outcome. Under Pontiac the Indians organized a confederacy to drive out the English and regain their lost lands. They destroyed the forts ceded by the French to the English— Presque Isle (Erie), Le Bœuf, and Venango (Franklin)—and laid seige to Fort Pitt. Colonel Henry Bouquet was sent to relieve Fort Pitt. On August 5, 1763, he met the Indians at Bushy Run (near what is now Export, Westmoreland County) and won one of the most important battles in American history. This victory cleared the way for settlement.

How the Settler Got His Land

III

THE territory now included in Pennsylvania had been granted by King Charles II of England to William Penn in 1681 and had been owned ever since by Penn or his heirs, although the people of the colony governed themselves. From the first the Penns had made every effort to induce settlers to come to Pennsylvania. They came by thousands directly from Europe—from England, Scotland, Ireland, Germany, and France—after voyages of from four to twelve weeks, during which a diet of hard biscuits, salt beef, pork with beans, and potatoes was common ship's fare. From the eastern ports they made the long journey to the westward, caravans of patient plodders along the rough highways.

Most of those who came were poor, some of them so penniless that they had to pay for their passage by signing an agreement to serve for a certain number of years with whoever would pay their fare to the ship's captain. These immigrants were known as indentured servants because the agreement they signed was known as an indenture. For many years the emigration from Europe of this class of people was encouraged by shipowners who sent out agents, particularly among the

German peasants of the Rhine country. The time of service was generally four or five years, after which these immigrants were free to go where they chose. Up to 1730 many of these redemptioners were British; after 1730 most of them were from Germany. The immigration of redemptioners into Pennsylvania reached its peak about 1750. When they had completed their periods of indenture they came in large numbers to the western country because there they could more easily establish themselves, since land was cheap and they could begin life again as free, self-respecting men and women.

The southern half of western Pennsylvania was first settled from Virginia and Maryland. Virginians and Marylanders were mostly Englishmen, although many Scotch and Scotch-Irish were included, who, on arriving in Philadelphia or Baltimore, had gone south through the Cumberland and Shenandoah valleys. Later these Scotch and Scotch-Irish came northwest into western Pennsylvania and took up lands in what are now Fayette, Greene, Washington, and Somerset counties. Many of the Virginians who hoped to better themselves by acquiring lands and making homes in a new region had been used to the open hospitality of the South. They were friendly and gay and liked good living, horse racing, dancing, and gaming. It was chiefly the Virginians who, among the early settlers in southwestern Pennsylvania, observed feast days and holidays, especially Christmas. The people of English descent who came to the other parts of southwestern Pennsylvania, particularly Westmoreland County, were mostly from eastern Pennsylvania, New Jersey, and Connecticut.

From 1720 on, many Germans settled in the region on each

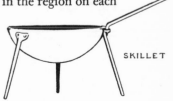

SKILLET

side of the lower Susquehanna River in Pennsylvania. These German settlers were industrious, frugal, and self-reliant. They were pious people with great love for order and for laws that they thought would maintain order, but they were also a superstitious people. After the first generation of settlement in the new lands, where schools and churches, books and papers were rare, many of them lost their habits of reading and writing or failed to teach them to their children, so that the second generation was often illiterate.

The Germans did not in general push so far westward as did the Scotch, the Irish, and the Scotch-Irish. The Scotch-Irish were so-called because they were of that group of Scotch people who had removed to northern Ireland two or three generations before their emigration to America. The Scotch and Scotch-Irish settlers had inherited the political ideas and religious teachings of John Knox and Andrew Melville. They were chiefly Calvinists, whose preachers in the old country had taught them the ideal of the freedom of the individual. There, too, they had been forbidden to trade with England's colonies because England wanted that trade for her own manufacturers, and as a result most of their seaports were ruined; land values dropped, and the tenants became impoverished. Many of these people scraped together enough money to buy passage to America, or they agreed to become indentured servants. It was said that land was cheap in the western country and that there was room there for men's consciences to work.

The Scotch, the Irish, and the Scotch-Irish did not get along well with the Quakers of eastern Pennsylvania and so were pushed out to the frontiers, farther west than the region where the Germans settled. They were more aggressive than the Germans. They were more restless, too, harsher and less tolerant, easily angered and as easily won to friendship. They were hardy, and were able drinkers and fighters. They sometimes settled on lands still belonging to the Indians, much to the alarm of the red men.

Some Welsh also settled in Pennsylvania and some of them moved to Cambria County. And there were more French Huguenots in Pennsylvania than in any other state north of the Carolinas, although most of them kept to the eastern part of the state. A number of individual families of French Huguenots, however, who had migrated from France to Germany during the French persecutions of the Protestants, drifted through to the West with the Germans.

The early population of western Pennsylvania has usually been spoken of as chiefly Scotch-Irish, but recent studies show that there were really more of the English than of any other nationality. Perhaps the fiery energy and the quick temperament of the Scotch-Irish made them seem greater in number than other groups of settlers. Then, too, they were always in the fore of all fights that took place, whether in the intimacy of the taverns or in group uprisings such as the Whiskey Insurrection. They were also most prominent in the religious development of the new communities.

During and immediately following the Revolutionary War many who did not want to fight came from the eastern counties into the western end of the state. These citizens of the East, who had refused to join in what seemed to them a civil war or who had actively sided with the King and felt that the colo-

CALABASHES

nies should not secede from the mother country, aroused the hostility of the eastern patriots. Many of them were arrested, sometimes paroled and sometimes exiled. After the British gave up Philadelphia in 1778, feeling against these "traitors" ran so high that they were fined or imprisoned; their properties were taken over by the state; their lands and their homes sold at auction. To escape such hardships they moved westward. They and the newly freed indentured servants were, on the whole, extremely poor, but they were hopeful of the advantages of the frontier.

HANGING
GRIDDLE

Land speculators came for other reasons. Their business was to buy up tracts of land and to sell them to settlers. They advertised the country, organized settlement companies, and had laws passed to make settlement easy. Washington was one of the greatest of these speculators and was the closest rival of the man who was perhaps the greatest of them all before the Revolution, George Croghan.

Thus during the last forty years of the eighteenth century the western country was settled by the former inhabitants of the Rhine country and of the British Isles who found themselves reduced to servitude and who wished to regain their self-respect; by the citizens who could not side with the colonists breaking from their mother country and who were called traitors by their neighbors; by the land speculators who hoped to create great fortunes in the new country; and by adventurers, restless wanderers, and homeseekers.

When the first military expeditions were made into the region during the French and Indian War, need was felt for supply stations at which the army could replenish its stores.

Settlements along the line of march would serve as hostelries or inns for men and horses and as storehouses where supplies might be held in readiness. In order to hasten settlement, therefore, army commanders granted permits to families that wished to settle. These permits were necessary because the rights to this land had not yet been purchased from the Indians. The permits gave the settlers the right to buy the land when it should be placed on the market. Later land laws gave settlers the right to buy the land on which they had built cabins and planted crops.

The ownership of the southwestern part of the state—Greene, Washington, and Fayette counties and parts of Allegheny and Westmoreland counties—was for years in dispute. Virginia claimed that her royal charter gave her control of this section. She had a more liberal land policy than did Pennsylvania, who also claimed the section. Virginia's policy, known as the headright system, granted fifty acres of land free to each family of immigrants. It encouraged settlers to move north and northwest of Virginia; thus, settlement was, until after the Revolution, advancing more from the South than it was from the East. Virginia was interested chiefly in the settlement of her province. But Pennsylvania was more interested in profit from land and therefore bitterly resented the occupation, by Virginians, of lands she claimed as her own. A brief struggle followed between the interested parties before the dispute was settled in 1780 and Pennsylvania recognized the rights of settlers who had taken up Virginia grants.

Meanwhile the colonies had declared themselves independent of Great Britain, and Pennsylvania felt that the ownership of the land should be vested in the state rather than in the Penn family. By the Divesting Act of 1779 the ownership of unsettled land passed from the Penns to the commonwealth, except for certain sections or private estates called "manors" that were reserved to the Penn family.

The spread of immigration had not been steady through the period of Indian wars and revolution. Hardy pioneers who before Pontiac's War had already established themselves on their lands retreated in large numbers before the warring Indians. Then with the coming of peace and comparative safety at the close of the conflict settlement began again. In the period between Pontiac's War and Dunmore's War (1764-74) the tide of settlers flowed in through the mountain passes, chiefly into Fayette County. Those who had fled from southern Westmoreland County now returned, or others took their places, and when the Indians gave up more of their land at the treaty of Fort Stanwix in 1768 the movement was in full swing. During the troubled years of the Revolutionary War there was some slowing up of settlement. The frontier had a double duty of supplying its share of men for the Continental army in the East and of holding off the Indians in the West. The Eighth Pennsylvania Regiment was recruited largely from Westmoreland County, and the Thirteenth Virginia Regiment from Fayette, Greene, and Washington counties. The burning of Hannastown in 1782 by a company of Indians and Canadian rangers is typical of what threatened all frontier towns until peace was signed with Great Britain and peaceful settlement could once more proceed.

During the Revolutionary War the Pennsylvania land office

had been closed, and no sales were made to speculators or to settlers. But in 1784 it was reopened. Quitrents were abolished. A man could purchase as much as four hundred acres in a plot on a single application. Land sold at ten pounds for a hundred acres. By a treaty with the Indians in 1784 and another in 1785 all hitherto Indian land became the property of the commonwealth. The price was set at thirty pounds a hundred acres.

There was much land to be had. Many early settlers paid no attention to the legal processes of taking it up. Those who simply went out into the wilderness and cleared land for their cabins without permission from the proprietors or the state were called squatters. Both Pennsylvania and Virginia made attempts to remove these unlicensed settlers from the Monongahela Valley because of Indian protests, but with little effect.

In the early period a great deal of southwestern Pennsylvania was marked off as tomahawk claims by hunters or land seekers on their way through the forest. Each established his tomahawk right by girdling a few trees near the head of a stream or spring or at the corners of the claimed area and by blazing one or more of the trees with his initials or his full name. Such rights were not really legal but in many cases were recognized, and on this basis sales of land were made. Many people who wished to settle on such tracts bought up the tomahawk rights rather than quarrel with those who had established them. Joseph Doddridge, who was a boy during the Indian wars and from whose *Notes on the Settlement and Indian Wars* has been drawn much of the information in this book, says of these rights:

WOODEN
MEASURE

"Other improvers of the land, with a view to actual settlement, and who happened to be stout veteran fellows, took a very different course from that of purchasing the tomahawk rights. When annoyed by the claimants under those rights, they deliberately cut a few good hickories, and gave them what was called in those days *a laced jacket,* that is a sound whipping."

The story of George Teagarden's fight for the claim to his farm in Greene County is typical of the settlement of many disputes over early land rights. Teagarden had married and had prepared to erect a comfortable cabin home on his land. His friends had gathered for the "raisin'," and there was much gaiety. In the midst of the preparations there appeared a man who claimed the land and forbade the raising to proceed. Aware of the only law recognized on such occasions, Teagarden challenged him to fight it out. The fight was fierce and bloody, but in the end the claimant surrendered, and the wounds of victor and vanquished were dressed by the young wife. The two families later became neighbors and fast friends.

The settlement of the western end of the state falls rather clearly into two periods. First the southwestern corner was settled—Fayette, Greene, Allegheny, Washington, Somerset, and Westmoreland counties—during the period from 1760 to 1790. After 1790 the northwestern half of the state was opened, and towns sprang up at Erie, Waterford, Meadville, and Butler. By that time the frontier had already passed into states farther west—Ohio and Indiana. By about 1760 settlement in southwestern Pennsylvania was increasing steadily. The first settlements grew up around the forts, because they gave protection, or along the Braddock and Forbes roads, because travelers would pause to purchase supplies or because the pass-

ing military expeditions would buy the settlers' produce for
the garrisons. The main centers of settlement west of the mountains and south of the Ohio River were at Pittsburgh, at Redstone (now Brownsville), at Stewart's Crossing (now Connellsville), and at the mouth of the Cheat River, where Point
Marion had developed.

Because Pittsburgh was the most important military and
trading post, there was a town there from the first. In July,
1760, it had a population of 149, not including the soldiers
at the fort. Nine months later the population had grown to
332. In 1763 the houses of the town were torn down to prevent
the Indian besiegers of Fort Pitt from using them for shelter,
and the next year when the town was rebuilt the new town plan
of Colonel John Campbell laid out the blocks bounded by
what are now the Boulevard of the Allies and Water, Ferry,
and Market Streets. In 1766 the first shingle roof was laid on
a warehouse by George Morgan for the firm of Baynton, Whar-
ton and Morgan, of Philadelphia, whose trading at the Point
helped the growth of the new town. Settlements were fairly
well established between Pittsburgh and Bedford during the
years from 1760 to 1763.

In 1760 George Croghan had begun to develop grants
about four miles from Pittsburgh. William Clapham had settled on a farm on the Youghiogheny near the site of West Newton. Andrew Byerly had begun what was perhaps the first white
agricultural settlement in Westmoreland County, near Bushy
Run. By 1763 fourteen families were living along the Forbes
Road west of Ligonier, and there were also about a hundred
families around Bedford, east of the Indian frontier.

The Monongahela Valley had become one of the main areas of settlement. Farms had been worked near Fort Burd at Redstone, at the mouth of Redstone Creek—some, at least, under military permits. A thousand bushels of corn were sent from Redstone to Fort Pitt in 1761. Fort Burd had been a center of settlement as early as 1759. It was situated at the crossing of a navigable stream and an extension of the Braddock Road and was an ideal point for transferring from land to water transportation the goods which traders brought to the settlers. It was this district, now Fayette County, that was the goal of most of the early settlers of western Pennsylvania. Here they settled first the bottom lands near the mouths of the streams; then they moved up the creeks to the lands farther from the river but kept close to the banks for convenience; and finally they reached the higher ground away from the streams.

Brownsville, Fayette County, had been laid out by Marylanders and Virginians in 1785, although Wendell Brown and his sons had settled near there in 1750. In 1767 Thomas Douthet and Henry Beeson, a Quaker who was a blacksmith and a miller, had founded Uniontown; by 1787 a courthouse and school were established in one building; there were a mill, four taverns, three blacksmith shops, five stores, and a distillery. Into this district many Quakers came after the war for independence.

In Washington County there was the town of Washington, founded in 1781. It was a way station on the road between Brownsville and Wheeling for traffic that was seeking the Ohio River. On Chartiers Creek the town of Canonsburg was founded in 1787, and by 1790 it had a mill, a distillery, a store a tavern, and a number of resident mechanics.

Modern Greene County had Muddy Creek, where in 1768 the Swan, Hughes, and Van Meter families had built their cabins. By 1782 Hannastown in Westmoreland County consisted of thirty log houses. Greensburg had been laid out in 1785 and became the county seat in 1787. There were a hundred families in the Ligonier Valley as early as 1772.

What is now Somerset County was settled very early. A number of Jersey men had settled Turkey Foot, now Confluence. German Pietists had laid out Berlin in the years between 1784 and 1787. The site of the town of Somerset was occupied in 1771 by several hunters' families. The town itself was laid out as Brunerstown in 1785 and was expanded by people from Maryland, New Jersey, and eastern Pennsylvania during the Revolutionary War.

By 1790 the population of southwestern Pennsylvania had reached eighty thousand. This was almost wholly an agricultural population, however, with an average density of fifteen people to the square mile. There were a number of towns, but none contained more than four hundred people. Of the present counties as we know them, Washington, which then included the present Greene County, was the most populous, with a population of 23,901. Bedford, which included modern Somerset County, contained some 16,100 persons. Westmoreland followed in order with 16,000; at that time it embraced the regions north of the Kiskiminetas River. Then came Fayette with 13,325, and Allegheny with 10,322.

Within a half century the southern section of western Pennsylvania, from a wilderness occupied by Indians, traders,

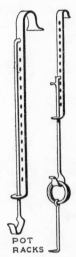

POT
RACKS

hunters, and trappers, had become a safe home for the overflow of population from the South and the East.

The northern part of western Pennsylvania was still, however, largely unoccupied, partly because of Indian raids that frightened off settlers from the donation and depreciation lands opened up after 1785. The donation lands were the bonuses paid to Revolutionary veterans of the Pennsylvania regulars. For this purpose the legislature set off a section of land consisting of the greater part of Lawrence and Mercer counties, the northern part of Butler County, and the western half of Crawford County. About three thousand soldiers thus obtained land for settlement. But as most of the men were desperate for ready money they sold their lands to speculators.

Another section was set off to be bought by soldiers with the Continental certificates which they had received as pay and which had lost most of their value because Congress had been unable to redeem them with gold and silver. Land that could be bought with these certificates lay in Allegheny, Beaver, Butler, Lawrence, and Armstrong counties. Even at the price of twenty cents an acre, less than half these lands were sold by 1787. Several large land companies bought up rights to the northern half of western Pennsylvania from the state. The North American Company, controlled by Robert Morris; the Pennsylvania Population Company, directed by John Nicholson; and the Holland Land Company owned most of the region among themselves.

After the Land Law of 1792, which confirmed the rights of the squatters to the land they had cleared, settlers began to move into this section. In a few years the northern half of that region of Pennsylvania west of the Appalachians was added to the southern section as a new conquest for civilization.

Settlement had now reached that stage at which purely agricultural living was giving way to the beginnings of industry. One early industry, of importance to western Pennsylvania farmers, was the distilling of whiskey from grain. Rye, which was largely cultivated in the region, had neither home nor foreign market. It could not easily be packed across the mountains. A horse carried only four bushels of it as grain, but distilled into liquor, which found a ready market east of the mountains, the equivalent of twenty-four bushels could be carried. This meant that whiskey could be transported at one-sixth the cost of transporting grain. Monongahela whiskey was the best in the country and was preferred in every market. Thus, when the long arm of the United States government at Philadelphia reached over the mountains and directly touched the western farmers with an excise tax on their most important product, great resentment showed itself. The frontier people felt that the government had until now more or less ignored them and had neither protected their frontier nor paid the militiamen for their services. There was little money in circulation on the frontier and since the tax was to be paid in gold or silver they felt they could not pay it. The tax seemed to them the hateful work of eastern industrialists and financiers, encouraged by Alexander Hamilton. Their distance from the seat of government, together with the feeling that they knew best what was needed in the West, encouraged resistance.

In the summer of 1794 the rebellious farmers tarred and feathered several of the excisemen, marched on General John

Neville's home to demand the surrender of his commission as inspector of the excise, and set fire to his buildings. Two weeks later several thousand angry opponents of the excise gathered at Braddock's Field and marched on Pittsburgh. Fortunately, at the last minute, they decided not to attack the town but merely marched through it. In October the federal government sent thirteen thousand militia, who had been gathering in the East, into western Pennsylvania to preserve order, but the expedition was unnecessary. The insurrection, if there really had been one, had subsided, and western Pennsylvania farmers had submitted to the excise.

While the whiskey rebels had been meeting, protesting, and marching, General Anthony Wayne had won a victory over the Indians of the Northwest Territory and by removing the danger of their raids had opened up a large part of Ohio to settlement. Thousands left the southwestern district for the new lands, and while Pittsburgh began a career of great industrial development, communication and commerce grew, towns multiplied, and the frontier began to move westward.

The Cabin in the Clearing

I V

WHERE his ax had laid low century-old oaks and ash trees clustered with red berries, so that ten or a dozen of the fallen trees left a clearing of half an acre, there the frontiersman might begin the raising of his wilderness home. Or he might choose a section of bottom land near a river, where the ground was already clear and he could begin work on his cabin immediately. Many an immigrant, worn with climbing over the mountain trails, stopped perhaps at some hill point along a creek where there were no trees, not knowing the land was poor. At the sight of such treeless land, he thought, in his lack of experience, that much labor could be saved if he built his cabin here. He was not aware that a tract of this kind offered only the most scanty return of crops for his plowing and hoeing. On such clearings, also, many a pioneer family that arrived too late to claim a fertile area struggled through bitter hardships.

If the newcomer had chosen wisely, however, he spent the first few days in a temporary shelter of tree branches or a cave while he set to work to clear a space for his cabin. If the felling of trees was to be done by his ax alone, he would clear just enough space to squeeze his cabin among the trees. When the crude little home was finished the first clearing could be made larger as he saw fit. If he used the Indian method of felling trees, greater space could be cleared at once, enough for a truck patch and perhaps for the first planting of a cornfield. The Indians cleared land by girdling, or cutting away the bark in a ring around the trunk of a tree so that it would die and let the sunlight through to the corn planted below. Sometimes they felled the trees by building fires around their bases. The fallen trees were burned into suitable lengths, then heaped on a pile, and reduced to ashes. This work of burning fallen trees was often done by the women. In one day a hard-working woman could burn off as many fallen trees as a strong man could cut with a good ax in two or three days.

BLACK BIRCH

More than one family at this stage of its frontier history went back to a method of living as primitive as that of the Israelites in the wilderness. The Harmons, who came from Germany to Westmoreland County with nothing but ax, mattock, and rifle, lodged for the summer in a hut of boughs built against a rock until their cabin was ready. During the summer they struggled to get into the ground some simple crops for winter food and lived meanwhile on wild fruits and berries and on what game they could trap and shoot.

A log cabin was seldom larger than twenty by thirty feet and one and a half stories high. In its clearing in the forest, on the hill brow, by the roadside, or by the creek bank, it stood close against the earth. It did not pretend to be a house, but was an honest cabin made of the crude materials that were at hand. For that reason it was the symbol and has remained the symbol of American traditions. There was not a false note in its structure. Its walls were unpainted logs, round or hewed square; the spaces between were filled with plain rails or were calked with moss or straw and daubed with mud. Its roof was covered with split staves, about four feet long and five inches wide, of oak or ash that had grown where the cabin now stood. The chimney often took up one entire end of the structure and was made of mud and sticks, in the humbler cabins, or of stones from the fields. Sometimes one window let in light, a square opening covered with greased paper. The door, usually with upper and lower halves, was made of roughhewn slabs and was barred at night by a log rolled against it or by heavy crossbars. During the day a light wooden latch could be lifted from the outside by a buckskin string passed through a hole and hanging free to the rare visitor.

The interior of the cabin was dim, and was relieved only by grey light through the one greased paper pane and, in summer, by the path of sunlight that fell through the open door. The walls were darkened by smoke from the big fireplace, and to them clung the smell of cooking, of hanging hams and flitches of bacon, of drying fruits and herbs dangling from the ceiling. Against one wall the bed was built—forked branches driven into the ground with poles laid across them to support a mattress of oak leaves or of cattails stripped and dried in the sun. Beneath the one small window a table of clapboards resting on pins driven into the wall might catch some light. From the cavern at the end, which was the fireplace, the flame of a pine log might flicker and shake its light over the earthen floor, across the smoked-grimed walls, touching the rim of a prized pewter jug, swinging black shadows from stool legs and from the clothes hung on the wall.

Rude indeed was the frontier cabin; its comforts were scanty, its discomforts many. It was drafty, smoky, and badly ventilated; its interior was sometimes visited by rats and snakes; its blankets and bear rugs were often infested with fleas. The dooryard was barren and unkempt. Usually the yard was kept bare of weeds, however, for the taller and denser the growth, the more danger there was from concealed Indians. Home life on the border, nevertheless, was not all rudeness. Friends settled near one another. Relatives came out in groups to the western border. New families made friends with older ones. Community life developed. Friendship and affection kept groups and families together as closely as did danger and suffering.

As settlers multiplied, as they became experienced in building with the materials at hand, as they added to their tools and found more time for building, they constructed houses of different types. A census of houses in one valley mentions round log cabins, chipped log cabins, hewed log cabins; scutched log houses, chipped log houses, hewed log houses, and round log houses. The log house was a step farther toward the development of the clapboard house. The log house was built of hewn, or shaped, logs and was often two stories high. It had at least two rooms, sometimes more; and the chimney, although still outside and at the end of the building, as in the cabin, was of stone and mortar instead of mud and sticks. The floors were of sawed boards, the roof of oak shingles was nailed on, and the windows contained glass panes.

With the growth of settlement there came about the friendly

LOG HOUSE

custom of house raising. Neighbors within the area of a few miles, when they heard of the arrival of a newcomer, would set a day when all could gather together to help erect the new home. This was the important factor in the gradual improvement of the pioneer home. Many hands could build a better cabin than two hands could. Doddridge gives an account of such a raising:

"The fatigue party consisted of choppers, whose business it was to fell the trees and cut them off at proper lengths. A man with a team for hauling them to the place, and arranging them, properly assorted, at the sides and ends of the building, a carpenter, if such he might be called, whose business it was to search the woods for a proper tree for making clapboards for the roof. The tree for this purpose must be straight grained and from three to four feet in diameter. The boards were split four feet long, with a long frow, and as wide as the timber would allow. They were used without planing or shaving. Another division was employed in getting puncheons for the floor of the cabin; this was done by splitting trees, about eighteen inches in diameter, and hewing the faces of them with a broad axe. They were half the length of the floor they were intended to make. The materials for the cabin were mostly prepared on the first day and sometimes the foundation laid in the evening. The second day was allotted for the raising.

"In the morning of the next day the neighbors collected for the raising. The first thing to be done was the election of four corner men, whose business it was to notch and place the logs. The rest of the company furnished them with the timbers. In the meantime the boards and puncheons were collecting for the floor and roof, so that by the time the cabin was a few rounds high the sleepers and floor began to be laid. The door was made by sawing or cutting the logs in one side so as to make an opening about three feet wide. This opening was secured by upright pieces of timber about three inches thick through which holes were bored into the ends of the logs for the purpose of pinning them fast. A similar opening, but wider, was made at the end for the chimney. This was built of logs and made large to admit of a back and jambs of stone. At the square, two end logs projected a foot or eighteen inches beyond the wall to receive the butting poles, as they were called, against which the ends of the first row of clapboards was supported. The roof was formed by making the end logs shorter until a single log formed the comb of the roof, on these logs the clapboards were placed, the ranges of them lapping some distance over those next below them and kept in their places by logs, placed at proper distances upon them.

"The roof and sometimes the floor were finished on the same day of the raising. A third day was commonly spent by a few carpenters in leveling off the floor, making a clapboard door and a table. . . .

"In the meantime masons were at work. With the heart pieces of the timber of which the clapboards were made, they made billets for chunking up the cracks between the logs of the cabin and chimney, a large bed of mortar was made for daubing up those cracks; a few stones formed the back and jambs of the chimney."

FIREPLACE

Signs of home and daily living gradually appeared—spoons of clamshells set in split sticks, gourds for bowls or dippers or

skimmers, and turkey-wing brushes for sweeping the hearth.
The plain Saxon names of many old household articles are
strange to us now, forgotten like so many of the objects they
belong to because these objects have long ago passed out of
use: piggins, noggins, trenchers, runlets, keelers, firkins, cowles,
and jacks. The frontier age was an age of wood, and many of
these objects were "turned" from ash knots or coopered from
staves and metal bands.

Iron was the frontier metal, and around the cabin hearth
clustered ironware of curious shapes and uses. Those who could
afford them used andirons in the fireplace to hold the logs.
From the chimney was suspended an iron hook, or trammel, for
iron pots that cooked a whole dinner at once. Other pothooks
of various sizes were screwed into the chimney place or hung
from a pole set inside the opening. Jacks and spits for suspend-
ing and turning a roast also hung from the chimney piece.
Sometimes a swinging crane was hinged inside the chimney,
or outside below the mantelpiece. On the hearth stood an
array of iron utensils whose shapes and uses would puzzle the
housewife of today. Since many of these articles were to be
used over the fire, they were made with feet to raise them
above the flames. Those without feet could be used on a trivet,
a small three-footed iron stand. In the better equipped cabins
there were gridirons, skillets or spiders, broilers for rabbits
and small game, braziers, and waffle irons. Pots and pans, waffle
irons, and all other utensils that did not hang from hooks were
very long-handled to protect the hands from the heat. Round
the outside of the fireplace might be hung other iron articles:
smoking tongs to lift a live coal from the hearth to a smoker's

TRAMMEL

pipe, long-handled toasting forks, and perhaps a brass bed-warming pan. Occasionally knives and forks were brought from the East, along with a few pewter spoons. Sometimes, if the settler prospered, he bought these from a peddler. Few settlers, however, could afford pewter dishes and spoons in their first months on the border.

Sweeping and scrubbing were done with split brooms; the making of them occupied many a frontier boy during a rainy day or a long winter evening. The end of a small hickory sapling was split for eight or ten inches by a jackknife pressed with the right thumb; the strips were bent back and held down with the left hand. As the splits were cut deeper into the heart of the sapling they became more and more brittle, until they had to be cut off. They were then turned forward and tied firmly with a tow string, and the pole above was cut to the size of a handle. "Scrubs" for scouring the table and the wooden trenchers and bowls were short hand-brooms, made like the split brooms but from smaller saplings.

The usual working day about the cabin began when the first morning light found its way through the forests and through the single window. If the appointed day's tasks were unfinished by nightfall, working hours were not easily extended, for artificial light was exceedingly dim and smoky. Rushlights were good enough at first, made of dried rushes dipped in grease. Or candlewood was used—pieces of resinous pine cut and dried during the winter. Strips of hickory bark were sometimes lighted and stuck in the cracks of the walls. It was the chore of many a frontier child to search the woods every evening for seasoned sticks and strips of shellbark hickory

TOASTER

for lights. The pith of cane and similar reeds was soaked in fat and held by tongs or clips, or stuck on an iron pin or a candle hook hung from the wall.

Although in the earliest cabins candles were a luxury, somewhere near the hearth might stand a candle mold, which consisted of a cluster of metal tubes on a metal base. In the poorer cabin might be found a set of candle dips, a set of long and short rods that was kept on a shelf year after year and to which wicks were tied to be dipped into melted tallow.

The earliest form of lamp used on the frontier was the Betty lamp, which was in shape as attractive as its name implies. It was a small, shallow receptacle, two or three inches in diameter and an inch or so in depth, shaped much like an antique Roman lamp, oval, round, or triangular, with a projecting nose or spout. It was filled with tallow, grease, or oil in which was placed a piece of cotton rag or coarse wick, which hung out on the nose to be lighted. The shape of the lamp was more attractive than its light, for the wick dripped grease and burned with a dull, smoky, ill-smelling flame. The Betty lamp hung by a hook and chain from a peg in the wall, or, for close light, from the back of a chair.

BETTY LAMP

Until 1834 the only means of making fire was by flint and steel struck together. If the fire on the hearth was allowed to go out, and if a neighbor lived near, a child was often sent to carry home a live coal or ember on a shovel, or on a broad strip of green bark, or by tongs. If there was no close neighbor, the tinder box was used. Flint, steel, and tinder were kept together in a circular tin box. The box had two sections: in one section the flint and a bit of steel was kept; and in the other, the tinder, a bit of dry linen rag. On the upper lid there was a place to hold a candle to carry the newly-made light. A later improvement made it possible to get sparks by spinning a steel wheel by means of a piece of cord so that the wheel struck a flint fixed in the side of a little trough full of tinder. The striking of a light from such implements required a very fine skill, you may be sure, and often took considerable time. That is why some one was often sent to "bring home some fire" on a shovel.

In time comforts multiplied. New equipment, fabrics, and tools were brought from the East or were developed close at home. Once fairly well established and progressing, many border people left their cabins on visits and journeys back beyond the mountains they had first crossed as emigrants. On such trips acquaintance was made with old comforts and new luxuries, and these were brought back to soften the rigors of frontier life. Many a pioneer boy and girl on such a visit caught a first glimpse of a world strange indeed to a child who knew only the rough simplicity of the frontier. Doddridge describes his own experience:

"I well recollect the first time I ever saw a tea cup and saucer, and tasted coffee. My mother died when I was about six or seven years of age. My father then sent me to Maryland with a brother of my grandfather, Mr. Alexander Wells, to school. At Colonel Brown's in the mountains, at Stony creek glades, I for the first time saw tame geese, and by bantering a pet gander I got a severe biting by his bill, and beating by his wings. I wondered very much that birds so large and strong should be so much tamer than the wild turkeys. At this place, however, all was right, excepting the large birds which they called geese.

The cabin and its furniture were such as I had been accustomed to see in the backwoods, as my country was there called. At Bedford everything was changed. The tavern at which my uncle put up, was a stone house, and to make the change still more complete it was plastered in the inside, both as to the walls and ceilings. On going into the dining room I was struck with astonishment at the appearance of the house. I had no idea that there was any house in the world which was not built of logs; but here I looked around the house and could see no logs, and above I could see no joists; whether such a thing had been made by the hands of man, or had grown so of itself, I could not conjecture. I had not the courage to inquire anything about it. When supper came on, 'my confusion was worse confounded.' A little cup stood in a bigger one with some brownish looking stuff in it, which was neither milk, hominy, nor broth; what to do with these little cups and the little spoon belonging to them, I could not tell; and I was afraid to ask anything concerning the use of them.

"It was in the time of the war, and the company were giving accounts of catching, whipping and hanging the tories. The word *jail* frequently occurred: this word I had never heard before; but I soon discovered, and was much terrified at its meaning, and supposed that we were in much danger of the fate of the tories; for I thought, as we had come from the backwoods, it was altogether likely that we must be tories too. For fear of being discovered I durst not utter a single word. I therefore watched attentively to see what the big folks would do with their little cups and spoons. I imitated them, and found the taste of the coffee nauseous beyond anything I ever had

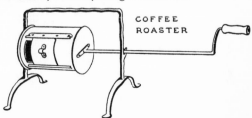

COFFEE
ROASTER

tasted in my life. I continued to drink, as the rest of the company did, with the tears streaming from my eyes, but when it was to end I was at a loss to know, as the little cups were filled immediately after being emptied. This circumstance distressed me very much, as I durst not say I had enough. Looking attentively at the grown persons, I saw one man turn his little cup bottom upwards and put his little spoon across it. I observed that after this his cup was not filled again; I followed his example, and to my great satisfaction, the result as to my cup was the same.

"The introduction of delft ware was considered by many of the backwoods people as a culpable innovation. It was too easily broken, and the plates of that ware dulled their scalping and clasp knives; tea ware was too small for *men;* they might do for women and children. Tea and coffee were only slops, which in the adage of the day 'did not stick by the ribs.' The idea was they were designed only for people of quality, who do not labor, or the sick. A genuine backwoodsman would have thought himself disgraced by showing a fondness for those slops. Indeed, many of them have, to this day, very little respect for them."

When the "genuine backwoodsman" had to start cabin housekeeping and to continue it as long as most of them did with a nearly or quite empty purse, it is easy to understand how he felt about the lack of comforts and luxuries. Families that started housekeeping with twenty dollars' worth of goods, or less, could not very soon have even the most ordinary comforts. John Reynolds, one of the early settlers of Meadville, wrote:

"More than half the people slept on the floor with their feet to the fire. I have myself so slept in a neighbor's cabin. The conventional customs of those years would be intolerable now . . . Nor was there lack of modesty where one room was bed chamber for all. One sex retired while the other disrobed, then the light—if any—was put out and the former returned and disposed themselves for sleep."

When they did retire, it was usually under bearskins. If the cabin contained a cockloft of loose planks, this was covered with straw for the younger members of the family, and their sleep was disturbed very often by scurrying rats.

But improved furnishings kept pace with the building of more substantial cabins. Cooper ware, well executed, was in time used for holding milk, water, and other liquids. Cedar ware, of alternate red and white staves, made its appearance and was thought very beautiful. Men learned to make set work, which was really coopering in miniature; for this the staves were all attached to the bottom of the vessel by means of grooves cut in with a clasp knife and a small chisel. Later, too, quilts were made from patches of outworn clothing. When calico and gingham became common, quilts were made from these materials cut into beautiful patterns.

As in all things, time was the softening influence on the roughness of cabin life. It brought knowledge of how to make new furnishings, and it brought money to buy them with. But in the beginning the frontier cabin was rude, and life within its walls was harsh. Nevertheless, it was the settler's home.

Linsey and Buckskin: Venison and Pone

V

FRONTIER dress was as much the product of environment as were the log cabin and the food of the settlers. These people whose bodies became gaunt and sinewy from privation, exposure, constant toil, and rough diet would ill have worn the fine fabrics and styles that prevailed in the fashionable world of the East. Plain, coarse enough to resist hard wear, and practical enough for protection, the clothing of the frontier men and women was perfectly adapted to its time and place. As with their cabins, their dress was the result of the materials and methods immediately available.

The men of the frontier, chiefly, adopted in part the dress of the Indians; they learned what was most suited to their life as scout, as farmer-soldier, as hunter. The hunting shirt, which hung almost to the knees and had a cape over the shoulders, could not have been more practical. Its color, if it was of jean or linsey, was usually tan or a red compounded of copperas and madder. If of dressed deerskin, its color was light brown. Its loose bosom, which could be lapped over half a foot and was held shut by a belt tied behind, was perfectly adjusted to the needs of a hunting trip or of a scouting expedition. In its fullness could be stowed a small bag of meal and a piece of jerk for the day, pieces of tow for wiping the rifle barrel, and other necessities. From the belt in the front hung mittens, in cold weather, and a bullet bag decorated with a squirrel's tail. The tomahawk hung at the right, and at the left the hunting knife in its leather sheath. Over one shoulder was slung the powder horn, protected by a square of deerskin. Breeches and leggings were of the same material as the shirt. In winter deerskin was cold and clammy; rain stiffened and cracked it. For this reason, linsey was worn in preference to deerskin in cold or wet weather. Moccasins were made of a single piece of deerskin gathered along the top of the foot and from the bottom of the heel to the ankle. They had flaps at each side that reached some distance up the legs, and these were strapped round by thongs so that dust, gravel, and snow could not work inside. Although such footwear was better adapted to frontier travel than heeled shoes, it was bad in wet weather and in winter moccasins had to be stuffed with deer's hair or dried leaves to keep the feet warm.

Each family supplied its own shoemakers and tailors. Those who could not make boots and shoes could make shoepacks. These were somewhat like moccasins, with a tongue to which the single piece of leather was gathered. The seam at the heel was like that of the moccasin, but usually a sole was added to the shoepack. All through fine weather pioneer families went barefoot. Children did so not only about the cabin but even to church meetings and school. The pioneer woman habitually carried shoes or shoepacks and stockings in her hand as she traveled the miles of rough road to occasional meetings. As she

CANDLESTICK WITH
EXTINGUISHER

neared the log church, or the cabin where the meeting was
held, she sat on a brookside log and put on her stockings and
shoes. On her return, when she got out of sight of the settlement, she sat down once more and took them off and barefoot
continued the journey home. Her stockings and those of her
family she knit from homespun yarn.

If the frontier woman could afford to pack among her few
household goods any bit of finery of dress, she soon found it
unsuitable. Stripped of color and fashion, border life must
have pressed heavily at times on the hearts of those sturdy,
courageous wives and mothers, and especially upon the heart
of the young woman who wished to appear attractive in the
eyes of the young man looking for a wife. Rarely was there a
soft frill for girlish shoulders or throat, or a bright ribbon for
the hair. There was not even a mirror to reflect the eyes that
grew moist wishing for such things. But the gowns of the women did not lack grace. In blouse and sleeve they took the
simplest lines of the figure. The skirts were plain, long, and
full-gathered about the hips. There was no ornament except,
perhaps, the large kerchief folded over the shoulders. The
dresses were made of homespun linsey-woolsey in solid colors,
blue, brown, grey, or butternut yellow—colors that softened

SPINNING WHEEL ·with time, as did the texture of the cloth.

So durable and so scarce was clothing that old dresses were
re-dyed again and again. They were often thought so valuable
as to be willed to another generation. The scarcity of fine
clothes for men is shown by the fact that in 1781 a certain mag-
istrate at Catfish Camp (now Washington), in Washington
County, who had been summoned to court and who wished to

uphold the dignity of the occasion, had difficulty in borrowing a pair of leather breeches from a neighbor who had also been summoned as a juror. There was only one pair of good leather breeches in the community. Another instance is recorded in the history of an Old Redstone church, where we are told that nineteen bridegrooms were married in the same blue coat with brass buttons. For years, even in the towns, clothing in general was extremely simple and plain, partly because rich fabrics, jewelry, wigs, ribbons, and laces had to be brought from the East; and the need was much greater for such things as salt, nails, powder, and bullets.

Boys wore trousers of tow for everyday wear, and for the rare occasions of church services, weddings, or community festivities a roundabout, or sailor's jacket, of fustian. Seldom indeed could a "boughten suit" with its under jacket of cheap marseilles be afforded. A boy's winter dress included a suit of linsey, a wool cap, mittens, and a pair of old stockings with the feet cut out drawn on over his shoes to keep out the snow. Girls' clothing was much like that of their mothers. The coats and bedgowns and dresses of the women and the hunting shirts of the men were hung in full display on wooden pegs along the walls of a cabin. In this way they helped to relieve the bareness of the room, and they told strangers and neighbors the wealth or poverty of the family.

The settlers of western Pennsylvania lived a rugged, disciplined life, much out-of-doors. Their diet was simple and coarse. The forest itself offered many foods. There was game in the woods, fish in the streams, and bushes and plants offered berries in abundance. Until chimneys could be constructed, and often in warm weather afterwards, cooking was done at a fire outside the cabin. Fats for frying were obtained from meat drippings, and the fat from bear and opossum was rendered into oil and stored in deerskin bags for many purposes.

FAT PRESS

Bread, the most staple modern article of diet, was a rare commodity on the frontier. It was no uncommon thing for families to live several months without a mouthful of bread, although a rough substitute was made from dried pumpkin ground into meal. And from corn meal johnnycake was made. This was originally called "journeycake" because it was easily made on a hot stone or in the ashes at wayside fires. As it was difficult to obtain alum and soda, frontier baked goods were heavy and hard. Later, when these articles were more common, cakes and cookies, breads and muffins could be enjoyed.

Indian corn was perhaps the most valuable single article of food known to the settlers. In season, a boy's first task in the morning was to pull, husk, and silk enough to roast or boil for breakfast. As meal, it was made into johnnycake and pone. For supper the usual dish was milk and mush. Mush was also used, if milk was scarce, with sweetened water, molasses, maple syrup, bear's oil, or gravy from fried meat. Corn meal was sometimes mixed with boiled beans and baked in cakes under ashes.

"Hog and hominy" was another standard dish. For hominy the hulls of the corn kernels were peeled off by soaking them until they became soft in a strong leach made by running water through wood ashes. The kernels were then soaked again and washed, and when used were fried in venison grease or with pork or eaten with bear's oil and sugar.

Frontier diet contained overmuch meat because game was

so plentiful. It was common to bag wild turkeys weighing thirty and forty pounds and so fat that when they fell from a branch to the ground they burst open. Woodcock, grouse, quail, and wild pigeon were to be had for the lifting of a rifle. Within twenty rods of the cabin a man could sometimes shoot deer, bear, elk, or squirrels. A famous hunter, Philip Tome, wrote that it was not unusual to see a drove of fifteen or twenty elk crossing a river and that in two days he killed four deer and two large, fat bears. Doddridge says that the children of his day were taught to look upon lean venison and the breast of turkey as "bread." But this artifice, he says, did not succeed very well, for after living for some time on such a diet they became sickly; the stomach seemed to be always empty and tormented with a sense of hunger.

Trout were plentiful in most branches of the Allegheny; perch and pike in the Monongahela. There were also catfish, sturgeon, and bass, as well as turtle and eel. Fish caught in the colder Allegheny waters were said to be firmer and better flavored than those from the Monongahela.

As salt was scarce, salt springs were highly prized by early settlers. At first, however, salt was imported across the Pennsylvania mountains. Later it was brought from the Onondaga Lake region, New York, and from the Kanawha River Valley, West Virginia. Large underground deposits were also discovered in the Kiskiminetas and Conemaugh region, but it was not until after 1812 that this salt could be mined and sold with profit. From the salt springs it was sometimes necessary to boil eight hundred gallons of water to obtain a bushel of salt. When purchased it cost three dollars a bushel; so it was used sparingly, and spilling it was really a misfortune.

Forest berries were the chief fruits of the settlers. On Sundays it was usual for large companies of neighbors to gather berries under the protection of armed men. In time of harvest groups of children and young people, under a guard, resorted to the fallen timber for the purpose of gathering blackberries, of which tarts, or small pies, were often made for the harvest table. The forest supplied other things good to eat in the way of persimmons, crab apples, hickory nuts, and black walnuts. Whatever grew wild and was edible was sought—papaws, wild plums, wild strawberries, blueberries, raspberries, and butternuts. Acorns, chestnuts, and beechnuts were also used, although chiefly as food for cattle and hogs.

PAPAW

Beverages were little used at meals for many years. Water was looked on with distaste for a long time. But since most of the settlers made whiskey, or since it could be traded for, it became a regular item on the household list. Everyone drank it: men, women, and children; farmers, ministers, and mechanics. It was often mixed with sugar, milk, and spices. Morning bitters were taken regularly. These were made by pouring the whiskey over wild cherries or other bitter fruits, or over the bark of certain shrubs and trees. It was usual to take a dram before meals, and a whiskey bottle and two glasses were kept on every sideboard in the region. A guest who was not offered a glass on arrival felt that the house was inhospitable. It was kept on the counter of every store, in the corner cupboard of every well-to-do family....

Tea soon came into use, although it was used in strange ways until the settlers became used to it. People at first boiled the leaves, poured off the liquid, and ate the leaves. One writer records having gone into a neighbor's house early one morning to see in a large pot over the fire a ham being boiled with a mess of tea leaves instead of usual greens. Bohea tea was brought over the mountains, like many other foods. And it was a great day when fathers could go to the nearest settlement "and returning, bring back, to the great joy of their families, meal, butter, cheese, tea, sugar, and other articles of sustenance regarded as luxuries of the most delicate kind." Many settlers had been accustomed to tea in their old homes and found substitutes on the frontier. Kenny says in his journal, "Gathered mountain Tea which we used commonly & likes it as well as bohea." Black birch bark, spice bark, and sassafras were also used for making tea.

Coffee was introduced after the Revolution. The fruit of what was known as the coffee bean tree was used a great deal where it was found. And by way of a substitute honey locust pods were used in the fall.

Maple sugar and molasses were in great favor. The *Pittsburgh Gazette*, which boomed all local resources, carried a notice in its issue for December 27, 1788, urging settlers to make more maple sugar:

"A German farmer, in Northumberland county, Pennsylvania, where the maple trees grow as plentifully as oaks or pines in many other places, made three hundred pounds of sugar in one year, which he sold to his neighbours and to travellers for 9d. a pound. From the value of these trees, and the many uses to which their sap has been applied, the new settlers have learned to preserve them with as much care, as if they were

apple or other fruit trees. From the facility with which they
may be cultivated, and the profit which can be had from them,
it is plain, that a farmer in an old county could raise nothing
on his farm with less labor, and nothing from which he could
derive more emolument, than the sugar maple tree."

The same issue of the paper published recipes for the making
of maple sugar into molasses, beer, wine, and vinegar.

As life settled on the frontier and cooking utensils became
more varied, more and more delicacies appeared on frontier
tables. An old recipe book of 1790 contains recipes neatly
written out for potato pudding, Sally Lunn tea cakes, bread
and butter pudding, plum pudding, gingerbread, hard wafers,
yellow cocoanut puffs, blancmange, sauerkraut, quince liqueur,
wine bitters, "pumcan" chips, clam soup, and "wonders,"
which we call doughnuts. Puddings must have been plentiful,
for there are recipes for puddings made with carrots, with rice,
with almonds, and with apricots. Other delightful sounding
names found there are whipped syllabub, cream cups, apple
fancy, quince cream, gooseberry fool, floating island, and snow-
balls. According to this book, those who could afford it lived
well, for there are given ways to prepare beefsteaks, veal cut-
let, lobsters, oysters, and eels, to fricassee calves' feet, and to
make calves'-foot jelly.

The German families of western Pennsylvania had a distinct and complete school of cookery that has survived in all
its delicious variety. They had also a number of hospitable
customs, one of which had to do with butchering and sausage-
making time, or *metzeln* time. When the sausage was made, a
dish heaped with eight or ten pounds of the meat was sent to

each of the most intimate friends of the family. Such a gift was called *metzelsupp*. The friends, in turn, if they lived near, sent hot soup and other delicacies to the family busy with butchering. If the *metzelsupp* was not sent to a certain neighbor, the minister promptly learned of it and he felt that something must be done to reconcile the offended families.

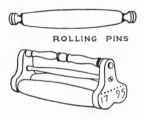

ROLLING PINS

Truck Patch and Cornfield

VI

A^S IN all young communities, agriculture was the chief
industry on the western Pennsylvania frontier. Upon
it depended all classes of people: millers, innkeepers, the soldiers in the forts, carpenters, ministers, lawyers, and doctors.
Many a settler had only a bag of seed corn with which to start
his crops; a little later he could trade pelts at the fort or at
the government store, or could barter a day's rail splitting
with a neighbor, for additional seeds. For the first summer an
acre of corn and a half acre truck patch was as much as he could
manage with the methods and tools at his disposal; and from
these he tried to harvest enough grain and vegetables to see him
through his first winter. With each spring sowing he cleared
more land until he gradually brought his full claim under plow
and sickle. Barring illness, Indian raids, and ravages from grasshoppers and other pests to which farmers were victims, he
could perhaps in several years produce enough more than his
food to barter crops for other articles. In rare instances the
military men might be supplied, and emigrants passing farther
westward, or his products might be shipped by pack horse
across country to the towns or to the rivers for transport by

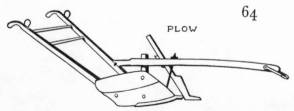

PLOW

boat down the Ohio. River transport, however, was risky because of the dangerous rapids, the leaky boats, Indian attacks, and river pirates.

The average frontier farmer who worried out a livelihood on the forty or fifty-acre farm he had cleared by himself, or with a few friendly helpers, seldom attempted to raise more than would supply his own needs. He lacked all but the simplest tools until he found time to make them out of the crude materials at hand; he was usually too poor to obtain them otherwise—at least in the first years. Improved methods that might have produced abundance were not available, and newspapers that carried articles on farming were scarce. Such surplus as might be obtained was usually due to good luck.

The farms of the settlers took the natural formation of the land as their boundaries—generally creeks or the tops of ridges, particularly the latter. Doddridge says that this is why so many farms in the western part of Pennsylvania had the shape of a bowl. This still holds true, for most farms are so laid out that the buildings are in a valley and the tops of surrounding hills are frequently the boundaries. Doddridge comments that our forefathers were fond of farms so located because, as they said, "everything comes to the farm downhill."

The farms in western Pennsylvania were, at first, generally fertile. Good crops were produced of almost anything sown, even with crude methods of agriculture. Maize, wheat, rye, flax, and Irish potatoes, in the order named, were the chief crops raised; and besides these there were buckwheat, millet, oats, barley, hay, peas, tobacco, and melons.

Farming methods were at best simple, at times very crude.

Farming was sometimes carried on with nothing more than an ax, a hoe, and a scythe. Most plows were of wood, until iron became common on the frontier. Men, women, and children hitched themselves to the plows like horses. Oxen, however, were used by those who could afford them, and later, horses were used. An early traveler, Michaux, wrote an account of his journeys through western Pennsylvania. "Planters," he said, "only plough the land once and do not fertilize it and never allow it to lie fallow." He observed that seeds were planted by hand and covered by a hoe or a crooked stick, that weeding and cultivation were done by hand and a hoe, and that in ordinary planting areas good soil and small size (three or four acres) made planting easy. Grain was reaped with the sickle or the scythe.

FLAIL

Threshing was done with a flail, an instrument consisting of a long handle, like the handle of a hoe, and another shorter strip of wood dangling from its end by a strong leather thong. With this, the kernels of wheat or buckwheat were beaten from the heads of the grain as it lay spread on a floor or on a patch of hard-tramped ground. A man who threshed out five or six bushels of grain in a day had done a good day's work. Sometimes this work was done by treading the grain with oxen or horses. Wheat was winnowed from the chaff by tossing the grain after it had been beaten or trampled with a paddle or shovel over a sheet spread on the ground. The wind blew away the chaff and the sheet caught the wheat grains. W. J. McKnight gives a vivid picture of the trampling of the grain from sheaves:

"The tramping was done by horses and by farmers who had good or extra barn floors. The sheaves were laid in a circle, a man stood in the middle of the circle to turn up and over the straw as needed, and then, with a boy to ride one horse and lead another, the 'tramping' in this circuit commenced. This was hard work for the boy; it made him tired and sore *where* he sat down. To prevent dizziness, the travel on the circuit was frequently reversed. One man, a boy, and two horses could tramp out in this way in a day about fifteen bushels of wheat or thirty-five bushels of oats."

The use of the cradle scythe made harvesting easier and quicker. Several slender curved bars were arranged above and parallel to the curved blade of the scythe itself, so that with each sweep of the implement the grain was laid in regular rows. In frontier grain fields men and women performed the beautiful, swaying, rhythmical movement of cradling wheat; at one broad sweep a space was cut as wide as strong arms aided by the long blade of the scythe could reach, and at the same time the reaped grain was laid in long golden paths.

The end of harvesting time was an excuse for what were called frolics. These frolics were family or neighborhood celebrations, when fun abounded. Any musician was called a fiddler, whether he played a fiddle, a fife, or a flute, or any other musical instrument that could be carried from cabin to cabin. There were reels and jigs and boisterous songs. The harvest had been gathered; the summer's work had borne fruit; the winter's store of food was pretty safely assured; anxiety was over, and people could forget themselves and their work in an all-night festival; they could be care-free and hilarious. There was no thought of having to get out early in the morning to the fields and gardens, for the harvesting was finished and the

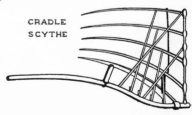

CRADLE
SCYTHE

morrow could be a day of rest.

When harvests had been gathered and the fall sowing completed the settlers took stock of their farms. Salt and other supplies had run low; tools were worn or broken. On the other hand, skins and ginseng roots had collected into a store that could be bartered for necessities. Or rye had been distilled into whiskey, and flax had been woven into cloth. Hence, families banded together to start a caravan over the mountains to barter such things in return for dry goods, groceries, and hardware. From among themselves they chose a master driver and one or two boys as helpers. Horses were fitted with wooden packsaddles and hobbles of hickory withes to keep them from roaming too far when the pack train camped in the woods at night. The bags that were to bring back salt were filled with fodder for the horses. Several bags of fodder were to be left at depots on the way for the return trip. When the men and boys had filled large wallets with jerk, boiled ham, cheese, meal, and any other food that would keep, and when the horses had had their bells attached and the clappers tied for the day—to be loosened at night when the horses were let roam—the little caravan got under way. Many a boy had the most exciting time of his life on such trips. And the men often visited the old settlements from which they had come to the frontier, gathering news to take back to their families and friends and carrying small gifts and letters. Such caravans traveled frequently during the autumn days between points in the Monongahela Valley and Frederick, Hagerstown, Old Town, and Cumberland, Maryland; or to Harrisburg and Carlisle, Pennsylvania.

Few frontier farms had barns or haymows. Wheat and hay

were stacked out for the winter. This was an art, for stacking had to be done so as to turn off the rain and stacks had to be balanced so that they would not be blown over by winds.

Every cabin had its truck patch—corn for roasting ears, pumpkins, squash, beans, potatoes, and cabbage. And turnips took the place of apples. One settler has said there was nothing more pleasant than scraping and eating a juicy turnip. Watermelons and muskmelons were commonly grown.

In the diary of James Kenny we read: "Having Planted out abot four Hundr of Cabbage Plants, there is not I think fourty left but what ye Grasshoppers has Eatten; they have serv'd them so in ye King's Garden likewise." Grasshoppers, drought, stampeding stock, and thunderstorms that washed out whole garden beds were not the only disasters to be faced. Frequently a whole patch of corn would be destroyed by raccoons or squirrels. Rats followed settlers to the frontier and became one of the greatest pests, destroying crops and killing poultry.

Kenny's journal shows another danger: "Through Mercy we were deliver'd last night, ye House having catch'd fire in ye Logs & was blasing up ye Clabbords & thro ye Upper floor touching ye Roof when I Awak'd & heard it, so was happyly Extinguish'd without allarming ye Neighbours." But not all fires were so happily extinguished. Frequently a family at work at the other end of the field would hear the crackle of fire and turn to see their cabin enveloped in flame and smoke. Often they returned from a short trip to a neighbor's cabin to find, not their hard-built home, but a smouldering mound of ashes.

Settlers learned early the value of Indian corn as a frontier crop. In the frontier soil corn yielded, with the moderate cul-

SINGLE YOKES

tivation they could give it, from sixty to eighty bushels an acre. It was food not only for themselves but also for horses, cows, pigs, and sheep. Ground into meal, it furnished the chief article of diet in the form of mush, johnnycake, and pone. The cobs furnished fuel, toys for the children, and pipes for the men. The husks were dried for bedding and for stuffing cushions. Several weeks after the corn had been "laid by"—that is, received its last hoeing—wheat could be sown in the cornfields.

Flax and hemp were important crops. Easily grown on any soil, the flax gave a pure linseed oil that could be put to many uses. The finer fiber was spun into cloth; the coarser fiber into tow. Hemp was raised for sacking and rope. The harvesting and preparation of flax was a series of laborious processes. It had to be pulled, threshed, spread out to dry, taken up again, and stacked. This finished the actual harvesting. Other operations that prepared it for spinning were delayed until winter.

Frontier winters seemed very long, for the days that closed in so early could not be lengthened by good artificial light as they are now. But there was plenty of work to be done, work for which there was little time during growing and harvest seasons. Winter was the time for mauling, or splitting, rails and for fencing. The mauling was boys' work, although strenuous boys' work. Blue ash was easily split with a maul and wedge, but honey locust was different. A boy could cut and split seventy-five rails of blue ash in a day; whereas forty to fifty a day of locust was a good day's work. There was a knack to mauling. The power of the stroke had to be well gauged, for the wedges flew out from a hard blow. Gentle taps were necessary to get them well entered. Boys did much of the fencing, espe-

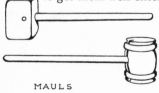

MAULS

cially the hauling of rails by dragging them with a log chain. If a horse could be afforded, the log chain was fastened around the ends of six or eight rails at a time.

Pioneer farmers were of necessity handy men, with some knowledge of several occupations, and they made many of their own tools. Winter days and evenings were spent by the cabin fireside getting ready a new flail, plow, or sickle for work that was still some months off in the future.

Every pioneer farmer who could afford it owned one cow, or more. The plentiful herbage in the unbroken wilderness made their care easy. The pea vine and buffalo grass offered good grazing. During May, June, and July, cattle were turned out to range, as well as the mares, colts, and horses not yet broken. At certain points salt was spread on the ground for them to lick up, and these spots became rallying places. In the latter part of winter, toward the end of February, when stored fodder had run short, cattle were again turned out to browse. For this purpose thickets of red or slippery elm were best, then white elm, then pignut or white hickory. When trees were felled, the cattle stripped the twigs and tender bark. Cattle had their ears punched with special "earmarks" for identification, and bells were tied to their necks so that their sound would guide whoever rounded them up. The bringing home of cattle and horses was usually boys' work, as was the herding of sheep. Another task for boys was sheltering lambs in winter and feeding them by the fire.

The more prosperous farmers hired men and women for much of the farm work. By the end of the eighteenth century farm servants were not uncommon; they were "washed, lodged, and boarded" and paid a yearly wage of from ten to sixteen pounds sterling. Men, women, and children became bound servants, or bond servants; that is, persons who signed a bond, or contract, for their services for a given number of years. Children were bound out by parents, by guardians, or by courts. When the bond was signed, to insure no mistreatment it was torn in two, and one half was given to the master and the other half to the servant. In case of complaint or argument between the parties these torn, indented parts were fitted together to display the contract. From the indentures on the edges of the torn halves came the name "indentured servants." This was the same method by which many of the early European immigrants earned their passage to America.

As settlement of the border became safe, many easterners who were at that time considered well-to-do crossed the mountains and took up farms. These farmers introduced into the western country good-sized droves of cattle, sheep, and hogs, because such stock could walk off the farm over the mountains to eastern markets. They cleared larger farms than the earlier settlers had cleared. They built gristmills and sawmills and distilleries, and they employed numbers of poor settlers. They could ship flour, bacon, lumber, and whiskey down the Ohio and Mississippi rivers to a good market at New Orleans. Hugh Henry Brackenridge, referring to transportation by water as compared to hauling in wagons, had said that people in the East, when they considered moving to the frontier, "calculated oftentimes that a farm in the neighborhood of these rivers, was nearer the market of any part of the world than a farm within twenty miles of Philadelphia." At New Orleans goods were unloaded from river boats and the cargoes transferred to seagoing vessels without payment of duty. This right was called the right of deposit and had been won in 1795 from Spain, which controlled the mouth of the Mississippi. But when Napoleon in 1800 acquired from Spain the province of Louisiana, which included the land at the mouth of the Mississippi, the western farmers were alarmed at the prospect of French control because France was strong enough to close New Orleans to western commerce and keep it closed. Eastern merchants, also, were concerned over the question, but they had a viewpoint different from that of the West. An open port at New Orleans would take much of the trade that might otherwise come to them. But in April, 1803, President Jefferson ended the dispute by purchasing Louisiana from France for the United States, and the Mississippi and Ohio rivers were opened finally to the trade of the western farmers. From this time on they could transport their wheat, flour, beef, bacon, and lumber down river to a good seaport.

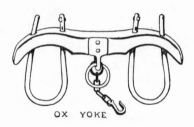

OX YOKE

Butcher, Baker, Candlestick-maker

VII

WHEN the cabin was built and furnished, the grain reaped and stacked, the pioneer turned his attention to other needs. Grinding grain; spinning and weaving cloth, which then had to be dyed and made into clothing; tanning leather for shoes and breeches; coopering buckets, tubs, and tankards; mending pots and pans; making plowshares, candle holders, and griddles—all these things were generally done by one family for itself. A pioneer family was a complete little world, supplying its every demand by its own efforts. In such practices lay the beginnings of the industrial empire of western Pennsylvania, which today satisfies our needs in a very different way from that by which the first settlers supplied theirs.

Near the doorway of every cabin stood the hominy block, a stump hollowed by fire or ax to serve as a mortar in which corn was ground by a stone, an ax head, or a sapling made into a sweep. One end of the sweep was wedged under the bottom log of the cabin or under a heavy stone. The other end was supported by a forked pole placed upright about one-third of the way from the free end of the sweep and serving as a fulcrum. To the free end of the wedged sapling was attached a piece of sapling about five or six inches thick, the lower end of which was rounded to serve as a pestle or pounder. Thus a person's weight would drive the pestle down upon the corn in the hollow stump and the wedged sapling would spring back after each stroke lifting the pestle with it. Sometimes a wooden crosspiece was attached to the pestle so that two persons could work, one at each side. When the corn kernels were soft, a simpler device was used—a grater made from a piece of punctured sheet metal fastened to a board.

In time the hand mill was devised, a distinct advance over the grater and the mortar. At each stage of development, pioneer life reproduced the long process of history. Each community was compelled to start from the point almost of savagery, but advanced quickly through each successive stage until it entered into the vast and complex enterprises made possible by the steam engine. The hand mill and then the tub mill were steps along the way. The hand mill consisted of two circular stones, one laid on top of the other; the lower one was called the bed stone, the upper was called the runner. These were encased in a hoop-like wooden ring with a spout for discharging the meal. A rod was let into a hole in the upper surface of the runner stone near its outer edge. The upper end of the rod, or turning handle, was so arranged that two persons could work the mill together. The tub mill was a water mill; consequently it could be used only so long as the spring freshets were strong enough to supply power. Not much grinding could be done by this method after May, for there was seldom enough water except immediately after a summer storm. Once the grain was ground it was sifted through deer-skins that had been dried,

SWEEP MILL
FOR GRINDING CORN

stretched over a hoop, and punctured with a hot wire.

At least a half acre of flax made up part of every frontier farm. It could be grown in almost any soil with little cultivation. After cutting, it was allowed to bleach for three weeks in the meadow, in dew, rain, and sun. Under this process the inner wood of the stem rotted. The flax was then raked and tied in large bundles and laid away in a dry place until after the fall wheat sowing, when it was completely dried out over a slow fire. The next process was the breaking of the flax. It was spread over a wooden frame, which had three blades of wood across the top and two more on a handle that was lifted from a hinge. As the hinged part was brought down the two blades fitted between the three. This broke the brittle fibers of the flax stems. The next step took it to the scutching board, where, with a kind of broad wooden sword called a scutching knife, it was cleaned of the broken bits of woody stalk. It was then hackled; that is, the fibers were pulled through the long, steel teeth of a comb called a hackle, and by this means the tow, or coarser fibers, were separated from the flax fibers. The spinning wheel then spun the tow into coarse yarn and the flax into a yarn of finer quality. The "scutchin' tow" was woven into cloth to be used for grain bags and coarser kinds of clothing. The finer fibers were spun on small spinning wheels into varying grades of linen thread for shirts and frocks.

SCUTCHING BOARD
AND KNIFE

As important as the tasks that made up the pioneer flax industry were those of the wool industry. Early summer was sheep-washing time; the sheep were taken to a stream or pond, plunged into the water, and given a rough rubbing. This was supposed to cleanse and purify the fleece before it was shorn.

When warm weather had settled into summer the shearing took place. Neighbor helped neighbor, proudly competing for speed but careful to shear the thick-wooled, wrinkle-covered sheep with the fewest "nicks" on the hide. Shearing was backbreaking work, for the struggling animal had to be held with one hand while the other hand used the shears. A skillful shearer removed the fleece so that it lay on the ground with its inner and whiter side up, almost wholly one blanket-like piece, which was rolled or folded and tied with tow twine. This might be done by hand or with the aid of a wool-tying table, which pressed the fleece into the smallest possible bundle. The carding of the wool into rolls for the winter's weaving and knitting was done by hand before the carding mill came into use. Each roll was a slender batch of stretched fibers from eighteen to twenty-four inches in length and as thick as a finger. These rolls were spun on the big wheel into yarn, which was scoured, dyed, and woven into cloth, which then had to be fulled; that is, shrunk and thickened. Some of the yarn, of course, was used for knitting.

When at last the cloth was made, it was ready to be dyed. Sometimes indigo was bought for dyeing blue, and madder for red, but usually the inner bark of the white walnut was used, and this produced the peculiar and permanent shade of dull yellow that was so characteristic of pioneer dress. The hulls of black walnuts gave a rusty black; copperas was used as a fixative when there was money to buy it, since it afforded a better tint for the black. Because flax was colored with difficulty and wool more easily took the dye, the typical material for a frontier dress was a linen and wool mixture called linsey-woolsey,

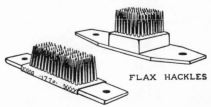

FLAX HACKLES

shortened in everyday speech to "linsey." For this, flax constituted the chain and wool the filling. In poor families linsey was often made of nettle bark. Every pioneer woman could spin, weave, knit, and sew for every member of her family. In sewing, the jackets and leggings of the men were more often than not cut out with a butcher knife; an awl served as needle, and deer sinew for thread.

Let a pioneer speak for himself concerning another of the early occupations. Daniel Drake, whose parents early settled in Kentucky under conditions not very different from those in western Pennsylvania, wrote that the most important manufacturing done by his mother and himself as a boy was soap-making.

"Father constructed the 'ash-hopper,' which was composed of clapboards, arranged in an inverted pyramid. In the bottom was thrown some husks, or straw, or dry buffalo grass, to act as a strainer. It was filled with ashes, on the broad surface of which the water was, from time to time, poured by the bucket-ful. A trough beneath received the lye, which, over a fire in the yard, was boiled down till it was strong enough to float an egg. The fat was then added, and the boiling continued till the soap came. By the aid of salt we sometimes made an imperfect hard soap, to be used for special purposes."

Tanning of leather for jackets, shoepacks, boots, and other uses was another occupation. A trough was sunk in the ground to its upper edge. Oak and hemlock bark obtained in spring from clearing and fencing the land was dried, and on wet days when work outdoors was inadvisable the time was used to shave and pound the collected bark on a wooden block. When the hair

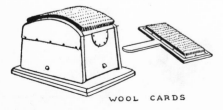

WOOL CARDS

had been removed from the hide by a lye made from ashes, the hide was soaked with the bark in the trough. It was then curried, or smoothed, by the turned edge of a drawing knife and finally dressed with bear's oil, hog's lard, or tallow. If the leather was to be blackened, the blacking was made from soot and hog's lard.

Sugar-making is also described by Drake:

"There were but few sugar trees on father's land, and he rented a 'camp,' as the grove was called, about two miles off. Our tapping was with the axe. The troughs were rudely dug out with the same tool, and generally of buckeye, as being a soft wood, which, moreover, was not apt to crack during the summer. One or two iron kettles, with the old iron pot, were swung over a log fire, before which was a kind of half-faced camp, covered with clapboards, as a shelter from the rain. While father did the wood chopping and kept up the fires, it was my province to drive 'old gray' with an open barrel on a sled, turning and winding through the woods, to collect the sugar water. Sometimes we staid all night, but generally got home before morning. In the best sugar weather the water ran only in the day, and when the flow had not been very great, we would bring the sugar with us. When it had, the 'graining' had to be postponed till the next day. . . . We took milk along, and made spicewood tea with the syrup; the time was that in which many trees and shrubs had begun to unfold their buds; the birds had begun to chirp and carol; the leaves of the cane were green; the wild turkeys occasionally paid us a visit; and, to top out the whole, we were laying in a good supply of sugar for the coming year, and I should add, of molasses, too."

MENS BOOTS

In summer, when the scanty flowers that could grow in the shade of the forests had sweetened the warm air sufficiently to attract bees, men and boys organized bee hunts. Sometimes a stone was heated, and on its surface a little honey was spread. As the sweet fumes rose the bees gathered, sipped their fill, and then made off in their proverbial straight line to the bee tree, where the men and boys who could follow the bees' swift flight found a rich store of honey. Honeybees were not native to this country, but always kept a little in advance of the white settlers and were called by the Indians the white man's flies.

Autumn brought the annual "killing," or butchering. Calves, hogs, and sheep were tied and thrown to the ground or hung from a branch head down, and their throats were cut. At the cutting up and skinning, at the grinding of sausage meat, and at the salting and smoking not only men and women worked, but also boys and girls—carrying hot water to the scalding trough, scraping the hair from the skins, climbing on stools to hold the sweet smelling hams while mother or father fastened them to the rafters. And when saltpeter for curing was available, children ground it in the hominy block.

Another autumnal duty was the making of a winter's stock of candles. A day was set, when, over a good fire in the chimney place, a kettle filled with melted tallow was hung from the lug pole or crane. Two long poles were laid from one chair to another, or from one stool to another. Across these poles were laid sticks of from fifteen to eighteen inches in length, called candle rods. To each candle rod were tied eight or ten strongly twisted wicks. The wicks, held by the rod, were dipped in the melted tallow and returned to their place on the poles. Each row was dipped in turn; the tallow on each wick hardened slowly between dips and the candles gradually grew in size. Too quick cooling made the candles brittle, and they cracked; so a good dipper worked carefully. On a good cooling day, when the room was not too warm, a good worker could make a stock of two hundred candles.

Candles were also run into a candle mold—a group of tin or pewter cylinders set on a base. Many an early household owned such a mold, usually of six cylinders, as part of its necessary kitchen outfit. The wicks were attached to a wire or a nail placed across the open top of each cylinder and hung down in the center. Melted tallow was carefully poured in around each wick. This work was often done by traveling candlemakers, carrying large molds that made sixteen to eighteen candles at a time.

Wax candles were made by pressing or pouring beeswax around the wicks. Deer fat, moose suet, and bear grease were all carefully saved in frontier settlements and rendered into tallow for candles, with the careful skimmings of meat drippings. If household labors were not too urgent, the frontier woman, on mild autumn days when the last yellow sunlight of the year fell over her doorsill, might enjoy a quiet hour while molding the candles that, burning, would fill the cabin with pungent fumes.

As candles were precious, they were carefully used and were kept in candle boxes to keep them from the light so that they would not discolor. They were burned to the very last bit by a small frame of pins and rings called a save-all. Many and various were the shapes and sizes of candle holders, from the hooks

CANDLE MOLDS

and sconces suspended on the wall to the candlesticks of many beautiful shapes kept by the fireplace on a special small table, called the candle table. Candle beams were crude chandeliers of metal or wooden hoops with upright pins or prongs upon which the candles were stuck. On a convenient tray were kept a pair of snuffers with which to trim the wicks, and a little metal cone, an extinguisher, to be put over the flames like a hood.

SLAW CUTTER

As kettles and pails and cups of tin or pewter became more widely used on the frontier, a new trade grew. Worn with use, bent, punctured, and cracked, these had to be mended from time to time, and the man who did this was the tinker. At first, the same head of the family who in summer had been farmer and in autumn had been butcher and miller and hunter now became tinker as well. With a simple soldering iron and some lead brought over the mountains (until a lead mine or two had been discovered) he patched up the house ware. Then when tin and pewter had become common enough so that the repairing supplied one man with steady work, the itinerant tinker made his appearance. He made his regular rounds on a pony, under him a pair of saddlebags that held his molds, his soldering irons, and other tools. At each cabin door he stopped to patch holes in tin cups, to make old pewter basins new, to cast new pewter plates, or to hammer out new basins on a block.

Coopering, too, became a pioneer occupation. Men learned to make staves and hoops and to cooper them into barrels, tubs, milk pails, and kegs, or into smaller articles such as tankards and noggins.

Rifle repairing took up many an hour. To straighten a gun

barrel all the frontier gunsmith needed was a small depression in the surface of a stump or a log and a wooden mallet or maul. He kept his gun in excellent condition at all times. There were also bullets to be cast, flints to be shaped, and powder horns to be carved.

Long, full days were those spent by the men and women of the frontier. And long, too, were the evenings. The sunny fields, the shaded woods, the stones by the roadside, and the creek that flowed back of the cabin all gave materials to be worked with, and the hands that grew hard and stained were often the only source of power. Although backs ached from a long day's labors with ax and knife, at the scutching board, or at the hand mill, yet night brought its own household industries: the carding and spinning of wool, the making of split brooms, the coopering of a new tub, or the tinkering of a pewter basin. Such household industries brought the family together, and while the logs crackled and fell and the fat-lamp sputtered, the big wheel hummed as it spun its thread; tales were told then of another kind of life. Each member of the family occupied himself with his allotted task, keeping feet and fingers employed, but the mind wandered off on its own paths, into the lands of long legends and adventures.

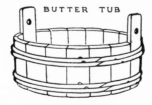

BUTTER TUB

Growing Up on the Frontier

VIII

"I KNOW of no scene in civilized life more primitive than such a cabin hearth as that of my mother," wrote Dr. Daniel Drake in recalling what must have been a typical day in the life of a frontier child. He continues:

"In the morning, a buckeye backlog and hickory forestick resting on stone andirons, with a Johnny-cake on a clean ash board, set before it to bake, a frying pan with its long handle resting on a split-bottomed turner's chair, sending out its peculiar music, and the tea kettle swung from a wooden 'lug pole'; with myself setting the table, or turning the meat, or watching the Johnny-cake, while she sat nursing the baby in the corner, and telling the little ones to hold still and let their sister Lizzy dress them!

"Then came blowing the conch-shell for father in the field, the howling of old Lion, and the momentary application of the shell to my ear, to hear the roaring of the sea, which, like all things in that fathomless profound, was a great mystery. Then came the gathering round the table, the blessing, the dull clatter of pewter spoons in pewter basins, the talk about the stock and crops, the inquiry whether 'Dannel' could be spared from the house, and the general arrangements for the day.

"Breakfast over, my function was to provide the 'sauce' for dinner; in winter, to open the potato or turnip hole, and wash what I took out; in spring, to go into the fields and collect the greens; in summer and autumn, to explore the 'truck patch,' or our little garden; and from among the weeds dig or pull whatever might be in season. If I afterward went to the field, my culinary labors ceased till night. If not, they continued through the day, and consisted of participation in all that was going on; now tending the child; now hunting eggs to boil; now making up the fire; now sweeping up the hearth, and putting things to rights; now cleaning the old iron candle-stick; now looking at the sill of the front door, to see by the shadow of one of its cheeks whether it was time I should put the potatoes in; now twisting a fork in the meat to know if it were nearly done; and now fetching a pail of fresh water, that father might wash his hands and take a drink.

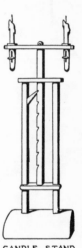

CANDLE STAND

"At night, all without being attended to, and the family collected, the iron mush-pot must be swung and supplied with water. Mother, or Lizzy (when old enough), generally stirred in the meal, but 'Dannel' often stirred the mush. This was, of course, a standing dish for the younger children, but father and mother drank their bohea tea (and abominable stuff it was; after a while, however, they reached the greater luxury of hyson skin). As often as possible, mother would engage in making pumpkin pies, in which, *con amore*, I generally bore a part; and one of these more commonly graced the supper than the dinner-table. At the proper season, 'wonders' made our supper, and although I never made the dough, I was quite *au fait* in lifting them, at the proper time, out of the boiling fat, and equally adroit in managing them at the table."

In the little community of the cabin clearing children were important citizens. They lightened the labors of both men and women. And at fourteen a boy was given a rifle and assigned his loophole in the fort, where he stood shoulder to shoulder with the men. A boy's life or a girl's was filled with chores that were half work, half play. Getting in wood, making fires, feeding stock, and going to the mill were parts of the daily round and could themselves have filled any average day. But these were not all. Other tasks were the grating and pounding of corn, bringing water from the spring, and carrying clothes to and from the pond on wash days. There was the churning, and the Saturday scrubbing and scouring with split brooms.

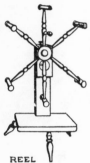

REEL

Children helped at all stages of woolen clothmaking from the shearing of the sheep to the sewing of the garments. Drake says that at twelve years of age he could handle the shears well in sheep shearing. And he comments on the picking of the wool when it was thick with cockleburs: "In this wearisome labor I have toiled through many a long rainy day, with my sisters and sometimes father and mother around the same fleece." The carding of the wool and the doubling and twisting of the thread was work in which the children could take real pleasure; the buzz of the big spinning wheel, as it increased in velocity, rose from the lowest to the highest musical note in the octave. Then came reeling into skeins and winding the yarn into balls.

In flax culture and in the preparation of linsey and linen young people took part. With father in the flax patch and at the swingling board, or with mother hackling out the tow and preparing the knots of beautiful linen fiber for the distaff, both boys and girls worked. Pulling, spreading out to rot, and breaking the flax were dirty and disagreeable tasks; but bleaching the cloth was pleasant and picturesque—spreading the linen on the grass, weighting it down with stones and sticks, carrying water from the spring to sprinkle the ever whitening material as the high summer sun fell upon it, until it was ready for making into new shirts.

Like Huckleberry Finn and Tom Sawyer, who themselves were survivals of the pioneer boy, every young fellow who could possibly afford the eighteen pence it cost had a barlow knife, a kind of one-bladed jackknife. Like the ax, the rifle, and the spinning wheel, the barlow knife stands as a symbol of those days before machinery turned out the necessary articles for daily life. Daniel Webster called the barlow knife the direct forerunner of the cotton gin and of countless other American inventions. It was indeed one of the most useful and most beloved articles on the frontier and was valued more than any other boyhood possession by generations of young whittlers, who, with it, learned their first lessons in making tools and toys. Not only were whistles, popguns, corn-stalk fiddles, bows, arrows, windmills, and water wheels carved by its blade, but also Indian brooms, scrubs, sled runners, hames for harnesses, thills for carts, hay hooks, pothooks, whip stocks, feed boxes, goose and hog yokes, spade and rake handles, stanchions, flails, cheese hoops and ladders, butter paddles, and birch bark baskets were all made by the boys' hands and the barlow knife.

How much depended for comfort on the right use of this knife! The carving of an ax helve, for instance, was a real art.

FLAX
BREAK

The perfect adaptation of an ax helve to comfortable use in the hand resulted in a beautiful object, for the handle had to be so sensitively adjusted to the shape of the palm that with constant use there was as little jar as possible from the thousands of heavy blows. Other things gave boys and men the opportunity to indulge their sense of the beautiful with the knife. Latches and long, heavy hinges of hornbeam were carved and decorated for use on shed and house doors. For doors and lids of closets and boxes, there were wooden knobs and buttons to be made, and in the cupboards stood many a carved bowl. Powder horns were also carved in intricate and beautiful designs.

Girls had their distinct share in the little industries of the clearing. About the hearth they were kept busy with skillet and spoon, stirring and turning and mixing. They helped bake the johnnycake. They peeled turnips and potatoes. They helped with the washing at the pond or at the hollowed log trough and with the milking and churning. Such tasks might be shared by boy and girl alike. But the frontier girl had her own domain, in which she was as supreme as a princess. At spinning, weaving, and knitting her fingers were as skilled and delicate as her brother's with his barlow knife. Stockings for all the family, mittens and shawls for winter, a pot holder of tow to protect her mother's hands from handles that grew hot over the coals, these she knitted at the cabin hearth or on the doorstep in the first cool autumn days. Sometimes the young women and girls gathered in the larger rooms of blockhouses, with their wheels and looms, to sing and talk together at their spinning and weaving. The truck patch was their

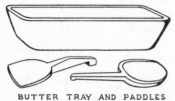

BUTTER TRAY AND PADDLES

special care, too. From spring to fall, while the men did the heavier field work, the girls helped their mothers with weeding, hoeing, and gathering the vegetables. And when the field crops were ready, if helpers were scarce or the harvesting had to be hurried in the face of threatening storms, they even helped bind sheaves and pile the hay into haycocks. But their usual harvest chore was carrying lunch to the men and boys in the fields.

Boys as well as girls wove shot-pouch straps, belts, and garters. A boy could make the necessary simple loom and could weave a belt in a day. A piece of wood about four feet long, an inch auger, spike gimlet, and barlow knife—nothing else was needed. A belt could be bartered for one day's work, or for the making of a hundred rails.

At the fall killing, or butchering, both boys and girls helped to cut up fat or to chop sausage meat and mincemeat. At the cheese-making they helped prepare the rennet to thicken the milk, squeezed the whey from the curd through bags, and managed the lever of the cheese press.

As in rural communities of the present day, winter was a period of comparative idleness for the men and boys. In most districts the roads did not permit sleighs, but rolling on the crust of the snow after a thaw and freeze and sliding on the frozen streams were popular with the youngsters. Released from labor in the fields, they were not willing to retire as soon as darkness came. But the light furnished by the candles or saucers of grease was hardly sufficient for reading the book or two the more fortunate family might possess. So in the winter evenings they huddled around the hearth and retold tales from

history and legend and sang songs of love and adventure. The
winter season also brought Christmas to some groups of settlers: the Germans, the Virginians, the Catholic Irish, and the
other non-Presbyterian groups. The Presbyterian Scotch-Irish
did not celebrate Christmas. From the little that is known
about holiday festivities, we infer that then as now it was a
time of mirth and gifts, especially for the children. Among the
Germans the Beltznickel Man, a member of the community
disguised in a panther skin with trailing tail, black bearskin
cap, and mask, romped with the children and filled their stockings with apples and nuts.

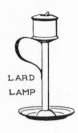

LARD
LAMP

After the snow and ice had disappeared, members of scattered mountain communities were more accessible to one another and could visit in parties on Sundays to sing hymns and
songs. Fishing also furnished diversion, and although with the
pioneer it was necessary as a means of procuring food, it was
nevertheless one of his favorite sports. Efforts were well rewarded, since the rivers of western Pennsylvania abounded in
fish, many of them unusually large; the perch sometimes
weighed five and one-half pounds and the sturgeon measured
four and one-half feet. Therefore, it is not surprising that fishing was a popular pastime for young and old—for the small
boy who caught minnows with pin hooks as well as for his
elders who angled for pike and catfish.

And for more exciting occupations in spring and summer the
boys helped clean out snake dens by firing them or by shooting
the occupants.

Sometimes a boy was left in complete charge of cabin and
clearing while his parents made journeys, perhaps several weeks

long. John Reynolds writes of his being left alone on such an occasion and his manner of recording the time that passed till his father's return: "Each day I cut a notch on the door cheek, and on Sabbath one of double size. Thus I kept tally of the days and weeks, and often counted the notches to pass the time which hung so heavy."

An important part of the boy's education came through his mimicry of calls of birds and beasts. Imitation of the call of the wild turkey decoyed that wily bird. By imitating the bleat of the fawn he led the doe to her death. To recognize such mock calls warned him of Indians who used them to signal one another for an attack. So by sportive competition the young pioneers were trained in a woodland art that not only aided in obtaining food but also protected the family and community from their most dreaded enemy.

For the same reason boys early learned to shoot a rifle, and, when the supply of powder permitted, all members of the family were trained in marksmanship. The boy was taught to aim at a mark by resting his rifle on a log or stone or against the side of a tree, so that the force of the explosion would not throw the bullet out of line. The young frontiersman practised so diligently with his rifle and took so much pride in its use that it was not uncommon for a boy thirteen years old to be able to hit a mark as he ran.

An arrow from the bow of a young brave would not have found its mark more surely than one shot from the bow of a pioneer lad. The more expert succeeded in bringing down birds in flight. And with what diligence a boy must have practiced throwing the tomahawk! He strides five steps backward

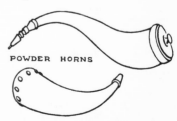

POWDER HORNS

from the tree, strikes the ground with the edge of his tomahawk, raises and hurls it. It makes exactly the given number
of swift turns in the air and plants itself firmly in the tree. Likewise the same trained eye measures the distance of seven and
one-half steps, and the tomahawk strikes the tree with its blade
up. His keen eye and trained hand can land the tomahawk in
any position he chooses.

When so many pioneer parents could not write even their
own names and could not have read them if some one had
written them, one wonders how so many of the children became not only literate men and women but doctors, lawyers,
professors, ministers, or writers as well. The parents were eager,
however, that their children be educated. The pioneer cared
a great deal for the future and for the future citizens of the
country he was reclaiming from wilderness. Every chance that
offered education for the children was seized, and as chance seldom offered, it was often created. Inasmuch as education is not
merely learning to read and write, but is also learning to think
and feel rightly about life, much of the training of young
people on the frontier came from sources other than school-
rooms and books. The constant useful chores performed about
the cabin gave children skill in many tasks. They, like their
parents, were trained by the conditions of frontier life to be
alert, resourceful, and courageous in hardship; and countless
influences bore on their sensitive natures—the quiet of forests,
the beauty of the seasons and wild life, the knowledge of woodcraft, the tales told round the cabin hearth. True, they were
exposed early to vice, and many crude ideas were implanted in
young minds from constant association with crude persons.

But there were also the visiting minister, the occasional visit of the doctor, and the pious and the educated members of the community, whose concern for schooling was strong.

Usually the first teacher was the pioneer mother, who by the light of the hearth, made a little brighter by chips thrown on the fire, drew her children to her knee and heard them stumble through their first letters and words. Often the only book in the cabin was the Bible. Sometimes a primer could be borrowed, dog-eared, torn, mended, and finger-smudged from use in other cabins. When enough settlers had gathered in a community, a minister who lived near might be prevailed on to gather the children together in a vacant cabin, or a cabin might be raised for a schoolhouse. Sometimes a widow or an elderly spinster knew the rudiments of reading and numbers. Men, of course, were preferred, for the teaching of frontier schools was difficult and dangerous. One case is known of Indians attacking a schoolhouse and murdering and scalping master and pupils.

If school was held in a room of an early courthouse, as it was in Washington, much labor and worry was saved. But there were times when pupils studied in the woods and recited in the cabin of the schoolmaster or mistress. The schoolhouse, however, was usually the "waste" cabin in a community, one deserted by its owner. If a schoolhouse could be built it was generally the ordinary cabin of logs, with broad puncheon floors, iron stove or stick and mud chimney, split logs for seats, pegs for the hats and sunbonnets and the home-made lunch baskets, and with the window openings covered with the usual greased paper. Along the wall by the windows were fastened boards on which the advanced pupils did their writing. Just inside the door, by a tow string, hung a paddle, one side marked "In," the other side marked "Out." When a pupil left the room he turned the paddle to read "Out," and when he returned, he reversed it. A law was passed by the state in 1790 providing for a school or schools in every county, but for many years such institutions were rare, and one school in a county could be reached by very few pupils.

WILD CHERRY

Although a minister might be found who could give some time to teaching, most children could not profit from such good fortune. Their foundation for the study of medicine, or law, or simply of newspaper reading was more often given them by a vagrant type of man who wandered into the community and, before many months had passed, disappeared under suspicion: a strolling Yankee, a questionable Irishman, or sometimes a roving Virginian—unkempt fellows who could teach spelling, reading, writing, and ciphering as far as the rule of three, beyond which they could not go. Of grammar, geography, and "definitions" they usually knew nothing. One out of many could quote a dozen lines of Latin poetry that he had picked up somewhere and of which he gave amazing translations. Most of the frontier schoolmasters had one talent of considerable social value: they could play a flute or a fiddle at the raisings and bees, and so could afford the cabin settlement some degree of extra service.

Schooling went "by spells," according to whether a teacher had come into the valley and whether the season brought little or much work to be done about the farms. A summer term was sometimes provided for younger children who were not needed in the fields or for odd jobs, and a fall term for older boys and girls who, during the summer months, worked in the truck patch, tended the cows, and helped in the grain fields and at grinding. Tuition was paid at the rate of a dollar and a half to two dollars for a term of three months, although those who could not pay were provided for by a poor fund. Many a log schoolhouse saw assembled on its seats youngsters of four and five among strapping fellows and girls, fully grown, who had not found schooling possible when they were younger.

The three R's—reading, 'riting, and 'rithmetic—was the average curriculum on the border. If a minister sat at the desk and held sway with the rod and the ruler, a little Latin and mathematics might be squeezed in for exceptional pupils. Occasionally some master came along who could take pupils beyond the rule of three, through the double rule of three, through practice, tare and tret, interest, decimals, and common fractions.

School was opened by the master calling out "Books!" Then the hubbub began. All pupils studied and recited "out loud" their spelling, reading, and multiplication tables, and the test of good reading was loudness and speed. The *New England Primer,* the *New Testament, Dilworth's Spelling Book,* and the *Western Calculator* furnished the meager knowledge that the pioneer youngster carried away from his schoolroom. This was made fast in his mind by frequent thrashings with birch rod or cat-o'-nine-tails. The hornbook, a single sheet of primer protected by a transparent sheet of horn, was in general use on the frontier, although it had long ago become old-fashioned in better schools in the East. The "setting of copy" for lessons in writing and penmanship was one of the most important tasks of the schoolmaster, and a boy who after six weeks at school turned into a fairly good penman was considered remarkably clever. It was a day to be remembered when the frontier child began to write "a joining hand and capitals," and soon he became of service to his neighborhood in the writing of letters and business and legal papers.

As in other frontier occupations, school supplies came from what materials were available. Lessons were written with charcoal on smooth shingles. Unruled paper and pencils were also in use. Maple bark, sumac, or white oak bark yielded ink. From goose quills the schoolmaster made pens for his students, and it was often his greatest accomplishment. As a reward for doing his lessons well a pupil might be allowed to make the pens.

Recess was unknown in frontier schools. But noon was a period of games in the "camp" or playground adjoining the schoolhouse, or in the sugar maple grove or the meadow across the creek. Many a homespun pair of breeches was ripped by climbing tree trunks in quest of birds' eggs. Many a knee was skinned and shin barked when two boys raced each other up the trunk, one on each side of the same tree. Black snakes were poked out of their hiding places under the worm fence by means of a stick, their backs were broken, and the limp bodies were hung over the fence to die with the sinking of the sun behind the hill crest. Girls were not excluded from the noontime games. Black man's base, three-cornered cat, town ball, and paddle ball enlisted every pupil in uproarious activity. At times a passing stranger on horseback interrupted the fun. It was the custom for boys, on entering the schoolroom, to remove their hats and make a bow; the girls curtsied. And when a stranger passed along the road boys and girls drew up in line and performed as a group the same friendly and respectful salutes.

The annual barring out of the master at Christmas as a challenge to distribute the season's treat was long looked forward to. The unlucky pedagogue, arriving at the door after his long tramp through snow that reached to his knees, found the door of the cabin school closed, the latch string within, and the pupils hilarious on the other side, toasting their shins at the open fireplace while he shivered and knocked for entrance. If he had brought with him a well-laden basket, his entreaties were shortly answered by the door swinging open and an on-rush of excited pupils. He took his place at the desk and from the basket laid out great pieces of gingerbread to be distributed when the excitement died down. He then dumped the remaining contents out, and polished, rosy-cheeked apples rolled over the floor to be gathered with shouts and laughter by scrambling boys and girls. The gingerbread was passed round, and the school settled down to sums and noisy repetition of multiplication tables mingled with spelling and reading. One incident is recorded of the master's turning the tables on pupils who had barred the door on him. When they refused to allow him to enter he set off into the woods, dragged a great log to the schoolhouse, and laid it across the doorsill. Then he laid another and another against the unyielding door until the shouts and laughter within died down as the pupils learned what was happening. He was about to make off through the deep snow homeward when relenting cries stopped him; the victorious master removed the logs, the door swung open, and he entered to start the day's session.

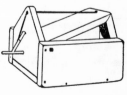

MOUSE TRAP

When the frontier boy and girl had picked up what odd bits of knowledge such schools and schoolmasters could offer they took up the regular tasks of farm and home. Boys often learned a trade. Girls had little choice but to perfect the usual home-making tasks of cooking, spinning, weaving, caring for the sick, and other wifely occupations. Childhood was not long on the frontier, and youth was little different from manhood and womanhood. Marriage came early, and with marriage a new cabin home began its own strenuous task of civilizing another corner of the wilderness.

Young people of the frontier were not excluded from higher branches of learning such as their cousins in eastern cities could study. Children of the more prosperous settlers were sometimes sent to eastern schools. Others who wished to pursue classical and mathematical studies, or those subjects leading into the professions of medicine, theology, and law, found opportunity to do so in their own district. Young men could read law or medicine in the offices of lawyers and doctors who had settled in the towns. After 1780 the Reverend John McMillan, the Reverend Thaddeus Dodd, and the Reverend Joseph Smith set up cabin schools for teaching classical and mathematical subjects. Then in 1789 an academy was opened at Washington, Pennsylvania. In 1791 the courthouse in which it was housed burned down. A lot was offered at Canonsburg, and there in 1794 the Canonsburg Academy and Library Company was chartered, which later became Jefferson College. Washington Academy was reopened meanwhile. Some seventy years later these schools united to form Washington and Jefferson College.

Before February, 1787, a log house in Pittsburgh had given

to the field in which it stood the familiar name of the "academy lot." In the log house for some time past young men had been taught the higher branches of learning. Now on the twenty-eighth of February, 1787, this school was chartered as the Pittsburgh Academy (which developed into the University of Pittsburgh) to teach Latin, Greek, English, and the "Mathematicks." Before long, penmanship, bookkeeping, and French were added to the curriculum. Here came the sons of the foremost men of the town, supplied with their own quill pens and their own candles for evening classes. And more than that, they made their own books by binding together the sheets of paper they had filled with notes at the dictation of their professors. Here, too, came young ladies, although at different hours from those at which the young men attended, and they entered and left by different doors. Nor did the young ladies and young gentlemen mingle in any other way at the academy. But the young ladies were taught by the same professors English, history, and French; "the Mathematicks," however, were considered too strong for their tender minds.

In 1794 a newspaper advertisement by the Reverend James Dunlap and William Littell, Esq., announced their school in Fayette County, where they taught "Elocution and the English language grammatically, together with the Latin, Greek, and Hebrew languages, Geometry and Trigonometry, with their application to Mensuration, Surveying, Gauging, &c., likewise Geography and Civil History, Natural and Moral Philosophy, Logic and Rhetoric." Here "boarding, washing, &c., may be had at reputable houses in the neighborhood, at the low rates of ten pounds [$26.67] per annum."

Thus educational facilities were improved little by little in spite of discouraging conditions. Pioneer children, through the determination of their parents and of other foresighted men and women, were able to obtain the fundamental, and later the broader, benefits of education.

WILD PLUM

Jigging It Off

IX

THERE came a late spring day on the frontier when a man and his wife, hoeing barefoot in their truck patch, raised their heads to listen to a strange sound. Somewhere back in the woods an ax was being swung against the trunk of an oak tree. Some one, not knowing how near he was to a cabin, was clearing a space for his own. A neighbor had arrived on the border.

Before the harvest was gathered enough cabins had been built within a day's tramp of one another to make a neighborly settlement. It had even been given a name. "Over at Evans'," people down the creek would say, "there's another cabin buildin'." "Up by Evans' town," a man carrying his grist from the mill would tell the miller, "I shot a bear on my way down here." Then, "Evanston folks are havin' a frolic, I reckon," the blacksmith would say as he shod a horse bearing a whiskey jug slung from its saddle.

No longer need the first settlers wish for a neighbor with whom to talk about what could be done for the cow that was sick or for the thumb that was festering. The frontier woman could now walk in one morning to one of several neighbors to help with a day's candle pouring. There were neighbors now to gather at intervals for a "praying" meeting. There were enough to make pioneer tasks easier by collective helpfulness— to clear a newcomer's land and put up the walls and roof of his cabin by nightfall; to make light of the corn shucking; to help in the fulling of the new weft of linsey just taken from the loom; to collect at night and make haste with the "bilin'" of the pails of maple sugar.

There were young people, too, who met once in a while for a kissing party. There was an occasional "marryin'," or a "buryin'." Even the burial ceremony was an occasion for companionship as well as for offering help and solace. The new family from over the ridge would be there, and some friends from the south branch. Not the briefest hour for companionship could be missed on the frontier.

General gatherings were still rare before the border was thickly settled, and bad roads often made attendance impossible, but border people crowded their pleasures into what hours they could snatch from their tasks. The long days of hard work were forgotten then in uproarious fun. The corn-stalk fiddle, the flute, or an old fife brought over the mountains carried the tune for rough voices shouting old Jacobite songs once sung in Scotland and Ireland or the Rhineland songs of the Germans. Rough jests and jokes were bandied. Great bragging went on, and tall tales of adventure. Stories of witches and goblins brought chills and bated breath. Everyone joined, men, women, and children, in jigging it off, jigging care out of the window and dark spirits out the door.

Sports sometimes collected the people for a festive occasion.

PATTENS

Usually late in the fall, after the harvest, a merry group assembled in a clearing or in the stockade to watch the men and boys compete in the arts of war and hunting. The mountains echoed their shouts and the reports of the rifles as they engaged in contests that demanded unbelievable skill. They ran races, vied in jumping hurdles or narrow streams, and, spurred by the cries of the spectators, engaged in wrestling matches. The excitement and pleasure of the day might be heightened if an argument arose or a long-standing feud came to a crisis that could be settled only by fists. As quarrels were common even in the simple society of that day, certain established rules governed fighting that reveal the vigor and fierceness of these people who had survived the rigors of the wilderness. Although weapons were banned, fighters were permitted to use not only their fists but also their feet and teeth. No damage that could be done by these means was forbidden, even the gouging of eyes.

Seldom did such a day end without some hatchet-faced braggart, pock-marked and huge-fisted, leaping from the crowd to a stump and bellowing his challenge. Perhaps he had spent some months boating from Brownsville to Pittsburgh or on down the Ohio to Wheeling, and in the rough river company had gathered their picturesque lingo. Hungry for a good rough-and-tumble and conscious perhaps of the power of such lingo to astonish his hearers, he indulged in it now in his challenge:

"I'm a Salt River roarer! I'm a ring-tailed squealer! I'm a reg'lar screamer from the ol' Massassip'! WHOOP! I'm the very infant that refused his milk before its eyes were open, and called out for a bottle of old rye! I love the women an' I'm chockful o' fight! I'm half wild horse and half cock-eyed alligator and the rest o' me is crooked snags an' red-hot snappin' turtle. I can hit like fourth-proof lightnin' an' every lick I make in the woods lets in an acre o' sunshine. I can out-run, out-jump, out-shoot, out-brag, out-drink, an' out-fight, rough-an'-tumble, no holts barred, ary man on both sides the river from Pittsburgh to New Orleans an' back ag'in to St. Louiee. Come on, you flatters, you bargers, you milk-white mechanics, an' see how tough I am to chaw! I ain't had a fight for two days an' I'm spilein' for exercise. Cock-a-doodle-doo!"

Certain games that could be played at the rare social gatherings furnished entertainment the year around. Corn kernels served as checkers and were also used in a game called "Fox and Geese." A lively frolic called "Hurly-burly" was a favorite. Two people went round and secretly appointed each member of the group to perform a certain act. This girl was to pull a young man's hair, another to tweak an ear or nose, another to trip some one, and so on. When all had been told what to do, the leader cried, "Hurly-burly!", and the confusion that followed gave the game its name.

Drop the handkerchief was a game likely to be played by the younger children on the edge of the party. The words of the song were not always the same. One form, much like the modern version, follows:

> Wiskit-a-waskit,
> A green leather basket;
> I wrote a letter to my love,
> And on the way I lost it;
> Some of you have picked it up,
> And put it in your pocket.

> I have a little dog at home,
> And it shan't bite you,
> Nor you, nor you, nor you;
> But it shall bite *you*.

Among the young folks the event anticipated most joyously was the "kissing party," so called because in all the games, either as a penalty or as part of the play, each girl was kissed by some one of the boys. These games were musical and vocal, usually performed to the strains of a fiddle. When all the guests had gathered and the cabin was swarming with giggling girls in blue and green linsey and noisy boys in buckskin hunting shirts, the fiddler struck up a tune, a young blade was dragged to the center of the floor, and the play began. The others joined hands and circled about him singing:

> King William was King James's son,
> And of that royal race he sprung;
> He wore a star upon his breast,
> To show that he was royal best.
> Go choose your east, go choose your west,
> Go choose the one that you like best;
> If he's not here to take your part,
> Go choose another with all your heart.

The boy in the center made a snatch at a buxom girl, and pulled her into the center of the circle with him. The singing grew louder:

> Down on the carpet you must kneel,
> Just as the grass grows in the field;
> Salute your bride with kisses sweet,
> And then rise up upon your feet.

At this point the girl was kissed soundly by her companion to the accompaniment of giggles and guffaws. The play continued until every girl had stood in the center of the circle and had been kissed.

Sometimes the play was reversed. A shy girl, her blushes heightened by firelight, her fingers hiding themselves in the folds of her linsey skirt, her long braids over her shoulders, was pushed protesting into the circle. A new song began:

> There's a lily in the garden
> For you, young man;
> There's a lily in the garden,
> Go pluck it if you can.

Encouraged by whispered hints and prods in the back, she pointed a shy finger at some lanky giant in red plaid shirt and bear-greased hair. For a few breathless whirls in his crushing arms her feet flew from the floor, her skirts and black braids swayed, and she scurried back to the circle of laughing companions.

To clapping of hands and stamping of feet the song went on:

> There he stands, the great big booby,
> Who he is I do not know;
> Who will take him for his beauty?
> Let her answer, yes or no.

Here was the moment long dreamed of by some saucy lass who had watched this fellow at the stockade, concerned too much with rifle and shot to feel her grey eyes upon him. She had carried him water and chunks of venison steak without even a "thank you." Here was her moment. She was the one who would choose him, flaunting her pale-haired beauty and the bit of blue ribbon her mother had hoarded for so long.

Song after song came from the playing groups, the old words and tunes of the Scottish and English folk songs that found voice for a time in the western wilderness about the Ohio and Monongahela rivers before they were carried on down the Ohio to the Kentucky mountains. The frosty night wore on, while the young couples, unheeding the wind and snow whistling around the corners of the cabin and the crackle of falling logs in the chimney, swung about the circle in laughter that often drowned out the words:

> Oh, sister Phoebe, how merry were we
> The night we sat under the juniper-tree,
>   The juniper tree, I, oh.
> Take this hat on your head, keep your head warm,
> And take a sweet kiss, it will do you no harm,
>   But a great deal of good, I know.

Then the rhythm changed and the clapping and stamping came quicker:

> If I had as many lives
> As Solomon had wives,
>   I'd be as old as Adam;
> So rise to your feet
> And kiss the first you meet,
>   Your humble servant, madam.

A rough screech from an old codger in the corner, whose memories had been roused by the evening, rose over the din of the youngsters:

It's raining, it's hailing, it's cold stormy weather;
In comes the farmer drinking of his cider.
He's going a-reaping, he wants a binder,
I've lost my true love, where shall I find her?

Dancing, of course, was a form of amusement heartily enjoyed by these buoyant people. Whenever occasion permitted
any number of them to be together, a tune was struck up on
the fiddle, and soon the floor of the cabin creaked and groaned
with the scraping of feet. Knowledge of only a few simple
dances had traveled across the mountains. The square set and
the three and four-handed reels were forms in which all took
part. In the heat of the evening, when the party was in full
swing, they pranced through the furious pace of the cut-out
jig or the Irish trot, the stamping almost overwhelming the
shrieking of the fiddle. When the dancers, tired from their
exertions, had retreated to the wall, one young dandy who
was able to outlast his fellows would leap into the center and
break into swift and startling figures of a jig of his own con-
trivance. In this way a party of pioneers frequently stamped
and swayed to the tune of a fiddle the night through. Often
the moon had gone down and the stars had disappeared before
the crowd, in couples and in groups, shouting and still singing
the merry tunes, groped along the roads and trails to their distant cabins.

Purely social gatherings, however, were not frequent. Raisings, marriages, and various seasonal tasks such as harvestings
offered the chief opportunities for amusement. If a new strip
of forest had to be cleared, the neighbors were notified, and a
chopping and logging frolic was announced. In the same spirit

of coöperation and with the same facility for lightening a task by making play of it, flax was pulled, corn husked, and apples pared for apple butter. Frequently the girls and women made merry while they spun flax, wove linsey and woolen cloth, and knitted stockings by gathering with their spinning wheels and looms in the spacious rooms of the blockhouses, where they cheered one another with song and sprightly conversation. And what hair-raising tales these pioneer women had to relate; Indian raids, midnight butcheries, captivities, and horse stealings were all within the range of their experience.

One of the hilarious events of the harvest season was the shucking party. Dr. Daniel Drake describes such an affair:

"When the crop was drawn in, the ears were heaped into a long pile or rick, a night fixed on, and the neighbors notified, rather than invited, for it was an affair of mutual assistance. A sufficient number to constitute a sort of quorum having arrived, two men, or more commonly two boys, constituted themselves, or were by acclamation declared captains. They paced the rick and estimated its contractions and expansions with the eye, till they were able to fix on the spot on which the end of the dividing rail should be. The choice depended on the tossing of a chip, one side of which had been spit upon; the first choice of men was decided in the same manner, and in a few minutes the rick was charged upon by the rival forces. As others arrived, . . . each fell in, according to the end that he belonged to.

"The captains planted themselves on each side of the rail, sustained by their most active operatives. There at the beginning was the great contest, for it was lawful to cause the rail

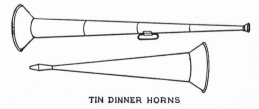

TIN DINNER HORNS

to slide or fall toward your own end, shortening it and length-ening the other. Before I was twelve years old I had stood many times near the rail, either as captain or private, and although fifty years have rolled away, I have never seen a more anxious rivalry, nor a fiercer struggle. It was there that I first learned that competition is the mother of cheating, falsehood, and broils. Corn might be thrown over unhusked, the rail might be pulled toward you by the hand dexterously applied under-neath, your feet might push corn to the other side of the rail, your husked corn might be thrown so short a distance as to bury up the projecting base of the pile on the other side:—if charged with any of these tricks, you of course denied it, and there the matter sometimes rested; at other times the charge was re-affirmed, then rebutted with 'you're a liar,' and then a fight, at the moment or at the end, settled the question of veracity.

"The heap cut in two, the parties turned their backs upon each other, and making their hands keep time with a peculiar sort of time, the chorus of voices on a still night might be heard a mile. At the close the victorious captain, mounted on the shoulders of some of the stoutest men, was carried in triumph around the vanquished party amidst shouts of victory which rent the air. Then came the supper, on which the wo-men had been busily employed, and which always included a 'pot-pie.' Such was one of my autumnal schools, from the age of nine to fifteen years."

Among the German settlers a common frolic was the *schnit-zen,* which consisted of paring about two bushels of apples for the apple butter "bilin'." The young men and women of the community gathered early in the evening to begin their task, and soon their fingers were working nimbly as they vied among themselves in the speed and neatness of paring and quartering the apples. As they worked they sang border ballads, told tales of witches, talked of strange characters of the border, and gossiped about their community. Later they were served with pies, cakes, and cider, and, when the apples were all pared, finished the evening with jigs and reels. Sometimes the boiling, or stirring, as it was often called, took place on the same evening as the *schnitzen*. In this case the guests gathered outdoors, where the great iron kettle filled with cider and quartered apples hung over a fire. They stirred two by two, a young man and a girl taking turns, while the rest wandered off in pairs under the autumn starlight.

CAULDRON

The fulling bee was a picturesque festivity for the neighborhood, one that possessed more folk quality, perhaps, than any other of the bees that enlivened community life. After cloth had been taken from the loom it had to be shrunk and thickened and softened. This process was known as fulling and is little heard of now because it is taken care of in the mills, before we buy the cloth. For the fulling party, or "kicking" bee, the floor of the cabin or of the largest room was cleared and cleaned. The material to be fulled was saturated with homemade soft soap and hot water and spread in proper thickness in the middle of the floor and surrounded by a circle of closely placed seats. On these the men and boys sat barefoot, with their trousers rolled above their knees, and grasped a stout rope that reached from hand to hand around the circle. At the word "Go!" all feet struck out at the soft mass of wet cloth, and the bee was on. Kicking and stamping, faster and faster, the fantastic dance went on in the firelit room. The group stopped now and then for breath, for the cloth to be turned and re-folded, or for fresh soap and water to be poured on. As the suds foamed and splashed and the cloth was flung and tossed and stamped underfoot, the shouts and songs and jests went on, with sometimes a slip that landed one of the fullers with a splash and a thud in the foaming, sudsy mass on the floor.

All these gatherings took the place of labor-saving devices of later years, for by gathering in all the hands of the neighbor-hood the labor was lightened and performed in much less time than one person or family could possibly have done it.

By far the gayest, the most anticipated, and the most purely social gathering of the border was the wedding. For the wed-ding frolic the settlers donned their best linseys and buckskins, laid aside their labors, forgot their terror of Indians, and, freed from the loneliness and isolation of their daily lives, indulged in merrymaking and revelry that sometimes lasted several days.

The celebration that accompanied the marriage of a pioneer couple in no way foreshadowed the hardship and danger of the life they were destined to live together. This life began early, for the bride was usually between fifteen and eighteen years old, and the groom, eighteen to twenty-one. Marriage on the frontier was very desirable for the woman. Her need for protection caused her to seek a husband early, and, if she be-came a widow, to remarry. This same urgent necessity for mar-riage was probably responsible for the wife's legal subjection to the husband. Until 1848 the common law of England pre-vailed, which decreed that the wife belonged to the husband and had no separate legal existence unless she committed a crime. She could not dispose of her personal property, which on her death passed to her husband. However, laws affecting the possession of property were of small concern in the meager existence of the pioneer couple. These marriages, entered into with so much revelry and continuing through the hazards and privations of those days, were, on the whole, congenial.

The wedding celebration began with the procession of the groom's party from his cabin to the home of the bride. This usually covered a considerable distance, and the young men, dressed in their best leather breeches, leggings, and linsey hunting shirts, the tails of their coonskin caps flapping, gathered early, since the wedding ceremony always took place at noon. Until the procession started, their horses had to be watched carefully, or some one not invited to the wedding might cut off the tails, the manes, or the foretops. As the party proceeded in double file over rutted roads and along forest trails and streams, it was hindered by fallen trees and mock Indian ambuscades, the pranks of the wedding jokers. Within a mile or two of the bride's home, the groom's party drew up in a starting line and, at a given signal, galloped off pell-mell over mud, rocks, and stumps in a wild dash to reach the bride's cabin. As the foremost rider neared the clearing, he gave an Indian war whoop and burst into the cabin yard amid the cheers of the assembled guests. The others followed, whooping and laughing as they came and the celebration began in earnest.

Everything was ready. Under the trees tables were spread with the wedding feast—venison, turkey, roasted bear meat, corn pone, honey, cabbage, all heaped in wooden bowls and trenchers. Treasured pewter plates the family had brought

COFFEE MILL

over the mountains might be in use for the occasion; there were a few iron forks, knives, and tin cups—not enough to go around, of course. Women bustled about iron kettles over open fires. The girls adjusted their linsey skirts and kerchiefs as the young man dashed into the yard. Children shrieked and tumbled about. The fiddler, his grizzled head cocked over the strings, screeched a tune above the hubbub, and the newcomers quickly snatched partners from among the waiting maidens and joined in the jig.

When the sun stood directly overhead, the bride was made to stand beside the groom under the appointed tree. The music and dancing stopped; the guests, still laughing and noisy, gathered around the bridal pair, and the person who performed the ceremony did his best to lend solemnity to the occasion. If a minister or a justice of the peace could not be found in the locality, the wedding was performed by the father of the bride and was confirmed by the first itinerant preacher who wandered to that part of the frontier.

The ceremony over, the crowd, jostling and shoving, crowded around the tables for the feast. The merrymaking was now in full sway, and above the laughter and the pranks played upon the bride, the fiddler screeched his tunes incessantly. A young fellow, watching his chance, snatched off one of the bride's moccasins and made away with it; whereupon her "waiters," three or four young men appointed to wait upon and protect her during the merriment, set off after the thief. The chase and scuffle that followed provided hilarious enjoyment for the onlookers.

The wedding festivities usually continued all night. When

the tallow dips were lighted in the cabin, the crowd gathered inside to begin the dancing with the square set, which was followed by reels, and finally ended in the cut-out jig. The dancers chained and circled, and the stamping of the feet grew louder. Voices grew boisterous. Songs rose and fell with the dancing.

A toast was proposed to the young couple: "Health to the groom, not forgetting myself; and here's to the bride, thumping luck and big children." This was indeed a wish for luck and prosperity, because children in the pioneer family were needed. The sons became the helpers of their father, in farming and hunting; and the girls aided their mothers in gardening, spinning, and other household duties. The toasts and feast over, the young guests "threw the stocking," to discover who would be the next bride. A stocking, rolled into a ball, was given to the girls, who, one after another, stood with her back toward the bride, and threw the stocking over her shoulder at the bride's head. She who succeeded in touching the bride's head or cap was the next to married. The young men repeated the performance by throwing at the groom's head. Then the guests gayly bade the bride and groom good  night. Gradually the dancers became fewer, the laughter less

CANDLE STICK

boisterous, the rhythm of the fiddler's tunes less rapid, and in the grey light of dawn the guests, many with their mocassins worn through, set out on their various ways homeward.

But the festivities occasioned by frontier marriage did not end with the wedding. The neighbors and relatives again gathered for the house raising. The men and boys formed a party of choppers to clear a spot in the forest. And while they set the logs and laid the floor, the women spread the feast tables. If work progressed rapidly it was possible to hold the house-warming the same evening; the fiddler struck up his tune, and the new home was heartily "initiated" with another frolic that lasted the night through. When the last notes of the fiddle had died away and the last departing guest had disappeared down the forest trail, the young couple had possession of their small cabin, there to begin life together. Another bit of the forest was cleared; one more bulwark against Indians was erected; a new white family had begun its fight for existence; and civilization had edged a jot deeper into the West.

"Indians in the Valley!"

X

TIME after time during the forty-year period after the beginning of the French and Indian War in 1754 fear and panic gripped the settlements. Bands of Indians swooped down on unprotected cabins to ravage and kill, to burn crops and cabins, to scalp, tomahawk, or take captives. Frantic, the settlers called for aid from the East. After Braddock's tragic defeat near Fort Duquesne in 1755 the provincial government took action; up to this time the assembly had been controlled by the peace-loving Quakers, but they finally withdrew from the assembly and left it in the control of those who favored the prosecution of the war. A chain of frontier forts was erected along a two hundred mile line between Easton, in Northampton County, and the present Fulton County, near the Maryland line.

There were few forts west of the Alleghenies up to the middle of the eighteenth century, but as the frontier line advanced it was marked by stockades and blockhouses; sometimes they were official forts garrisoned by the government, but more often they were settlers' forts thrown up for immediate protection. Between 1756 and 1763 more than two hundred forts and blockhouses were built in the western country. Fort Ligonier and Fort Bedford were erected in 1756, Fort Pitt was erected in 1759, and in the same year Fort Burd in the southwest. After 1777, several Revolutionary forts were constructed —Fort McIntosh at the mouth of the Beaver River and Fort Armstrong at Kittanning among them. The construction of these forts was made necessary because of the hostility of the Indians who, for the most part, had taken the side of the British. The Revolution in western Pennsylvania was not carried on by marching armies of blue-coats and red-coats but was a struggle between, on one side, bands of Indians equipped and led by the British, and, on the other side, starving and poorly equipped companies of American regulars and hastily organized bodies of settlers.

The important forts of the West were built according to the plans developed by military experts. Such a fort was usually square or five-sided with an arrowhead-shaped bastion at each corner. The walls were sometimes of earth faced with brick or stone and sometimes were mere log stockades. Inside the walls, near the top, were parapets or platforms, on which riflemen could stand; casemates, or bombproof shelters for the cannon, were built close to the curtains, as the walls of the fort between the bastions were called. Storehouses, barracks, magazines, and wells were located at convenient places within the fort; a drawbridge that spanned a deep moat led to the outside world. The bastions often enclosed brick or log blockhouses that rose far enough above the walls to enable riflemen to pick off skulking redskins that could not be seen from lower positions.

Outside the fort there was usually a village composed of

traders' cabins and sutlers' stores, and when there was no danger of attack a number of the garrison were sometimes housed in outside barracks to avoid crowding within the fort. The near-by forest was cut away to prevent besiegers from finding shelter in it, and for the same reason, whenever there was danger of a siege, the outlying cabins were razed or burned. Fertile spots near the forts were planted in corn and garden truck to aid in provisioning the garrisons, for it was difficult to transport sufficient food from the East to supply the hundreds of soldiers who were needed to defend the posts. The garrisons of the important forts were usually British or American regulars, although at times the province or state furnished a militia contingent.

The settlers' forts were usually ruder, less elaborate affairs than the military forts. The earliest type in remote places was the cabin fort, simply a large cabin to accommodate neighborhood families seeking refuge. It was sometimes equipped with a projecting second story, with openings in the floor of the projection to guard against Indians concealing themselves against the walls below. Narrow portholes were cut in the mud between the logs.

In more densely populated districts stations were built to shelter larger numbers of people for a longer time. A number of cabins placed on the sides of a square were united by a line of logs thrust upright in the ground so as to present a continuous wall on the outer side. The doors of the cabins opened into a common square on the inner side. Frequently an underground passage was dug from the yard of the fort to an outside spring. In some places the cabins were separated

ATTACK

from one another by log partitions. The roofs sloped inward for protection. At the angles of the fort blockhouses jutted out over the outer walls of the cabins and the stockades, with openings in the projecting floors. Entrance to the fort was by two large swinging gates made of thick slabs; they opened inward and were placed at that point in the walls nearest the spring, if there was none within the enclosure. Blockhouses and outer cabins were furnished with loopholes, and there were firing platforms built along the stockaded portions.

Around such forts were to be found the rangers, the type of pioneer who developed with a new order of life, when settlers were less isolated and had drawn together and adopted a system of defense. Rangers were organized into companies to serve for a limited time during periods of crisis. They also served as a kind of internal police within the settlements. Up to this time the idea of a fighting organization had not occurred to the settler. In the early years of settlement political organization and government—officials, taxes, and such things—had not yet been established. It was not long, however, until the frontiersman learned the necessity of acting together with his neighbors, of merging part of his personality in the community. Then the ranger as a type appeared.

The ranger was a kind of scout, a man who knew woodcraft and the tactics of Indian warfare. He was an army in one individual. He carried his artillery on his shoulder. He was his own commissary, carrying his rations on his back and replenishing his empty haversack with the rifle as the need arose. He not only was a match for the Indian in the Indian's mode of warfare, but he also had the advantages of organization. In

ordinary times—in times of quiet sowing or harvest, that is—
he might be a farmer cultivating his own small clearing. He
might be a trader collecting at various posts loads of peltry and
furs. But in times of sudden raid or when messages were to be
sent to a distant settlement or fort he was a voluntary soldier,
serving in a company or individually, and to him fell the defense of the frontier.

Every border man was at some time a fighter. The frontier
was won by the rifle and the ax, and the rifle was not the less
important of the two. If a pioneer could not afford a rifle, the
ax itself became his weapon, or the scythe, or any other implement that could be wielded defensively against a tomahawk
or scalping knife. But in every cabin where a rifle could be
afforded it held the place of honor on pegs or buck's horns
over the chimney piece, where it could be reached in that
second which on the frontier so often decided life and death.
At any moment of the day or night might come a thump on
the door from a warning hand, and the low call, "Indians!"
Then the frontiersman and his wife caught up their children
and the fewest possible necessities and scurried through the
woods to the nearest station or fort.

It was on the American frontier, rather than in Europe, that
the rifle was first used to advantage. Here reloading speed
could be sacrificed to accuracy and range. It replaced the old
smoothbore musket in hunting and war. Braddock's British
regulars used the smoothbore at close range. Many of the Indians and the French in the engagement used rifles from cover.

The loading of the early rifle was a slow process, although an
ingenious one. At first, a wooden mallet tamped the bullet into

FRONTIERSMAN

the muzzle of the barrel, and an iron rod jammed it into place, smashing it into the grooves of the barrel. Later on, the bullet, weighing about half an ounce, was made just a trifle smaller than the barrel and was wrapped in a bit of well-greased rag or deerskin called a "patch." This patch prevented the leakage of gas from the explosion of the charge and thus gave greater speed and accuracy to the shot, which no longer had to be pounded "out of round" in order to be gripped by the rifling of the barrel. A light hickory rod served to push it into place.

Rifles were manufactured in the East, particularly at Lancaster, the actual birthplace of the "Kentucky rifle." A man paid fifteen to twenty-five dollars, the value of a small uncleared farm, for his rifle, depending on its style of mounting. All border men devoted much time to repairing their rifles and making accessories and bullets. The necessary accessories to the rifle were the ramrod, the powder flask of metal or horn, and the bullet pouch. The powder flask was an object of pride and joy. It was usually made of cow or buffalo horn, the large end closed with a wooden disk about a quarter of an inch thick, kept in place by a close-fitting cap of metal. The tip of the horn was cut off to permit the flow of powder. The horn was often finely carved and painted and embossed with broadheaded nails, and the leather strap by which it was worn was likewise carved with curious and beautiful patterns.

The old flintlock rifle of legend and history was in use from 1700 until as late as 1850. A small pan of metal placed just behind the rear sight and above the end of the barrel was connected with the barrel by a very small hole. This pan contained the priming powder. Attached to it and sloping down into it

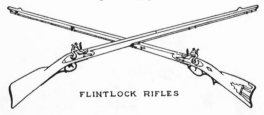

FLINTLOCK RIFLES

was a piece of rough-faced steel; in the final form taken by the flintlock this piece of steel became a part of the cover that protected the powder in the pan from wind and damp. The flint was attached to a lever, which, when sprung by the trigger, caused the flint to strike sharply on the steel over the priming charge. The ignition of the priming charge was communicated to the charge in the barrel through the hole in the bottom of the pan.

Doddridge's *Notes,* that pleasant classic of first-hand accounts written with an authenticity that a present day writer could only assume, gives an account of how settlers took refuge in near-by forts:

"The fort to which my father belonged was, during the last years of the war, three-quarters of a mile from his farm. . . . I well remember that, when a little boy, the family were sometimes waked up in the dead of night, by an express with a report that the Indians were at hand. The express came softly to the door, or back window, and by a gentle tapping waked the family. This was easily done, as an habitual fear made us ever watchful and sensible to the slightest alarm. The whole family were instantly in motion. My father seized his gun and other implements of war. My stepmother waked up and dressed the children as well as she could, and being myself the oldest of the children, I had to take my share of the burdens to be carried to the fort. There was no possibility of getting a horse in the night to aid us in removing to the fort. Besides the little children, we caught up what articles of clothing and provision we could get hold of in the dark, for we durst not light a candle or even stir the fire. All this was done with the utmost dispatch and the silence of death. The greatest care was taken not to awaken the youngest child. To the rest it was enough to say *Indian* and not a whimper was heard afterwards. Thus it often happened that the whole number of families belonging to a fort who were in the evening at their homes, were all in their little fortress before the dawn of the next morning."

Frontier forts were not only places of defense but were also temporary homes. Their occupants were not always garrisons of soldiers and scouts. During sieges they became little towns of one broad square—a kind of market place, drilling ground, and playground, as well as a pasture field for stock—busy with women in linsey gowns and kerchiefs and with laughing, tussling children playing games in the sun.

Women did much of the work about the forts. In case of attack they provided and served the men on duty with food and water; they chopped spelt, a kind of loose-eared wheat that grew on poor soil, for the cattle; and, with an armed covering party, they even ventured out to the spelt field beside the fort to gather the grain. They did the washing, gathered firewood, and cleaned the courtyard.

The small cabins packed with restless families were hardly comfortable. And the courtyard was little better, for here was herded the stock. Water became scarce, food supplies ran low, and the continual danger of attack wore on the nerves of the occupants. When it seemed safe, the families gladly returned to their homes and the men went back to their fields and clearings. But the anxiety of the women at such times became so great that many of them preferred to follow the men and boys to their work; they prepared dinner over a fire and kept a lookout for Indians, so that they might share the danger.

Forts were occasionally the scene of other than military activities. At Vance's Fort (now Coraopolis), in 1778, occurred one of these scenes. Settlers living near the fort had been driven, in the autumn season of Indian raids, into its walls for safety. During the long days and nights of the siege, a young man, Joseph Patterson, encouraged the settlers to huddle together for worship while some of the men stood guard with their rifles. In the smoky, ill-smelling fort he talked to the people tense with anxiety of a greater danger than that without the fort, of the danger of ungodliness within. He talked of a death more terrible than that by the tomahawk, a death in sin, unrepentant and unredeemed. Sometimes Patterson sat and talked with only three or four men and women, huddled on stools by the fireplace, while rushlights and pine knots sputtered. But in the narrow confines of the room his voice reached others than those gathered close to him—reached in fact all the company in the little fort. The group of armed men fell silent. Danger and the nearness of possible death drove home his earnest words. Patterson prayed. He led a hymn. Men with guns in their hands and women with sleeping babies in their arms joined with him. "The Lord was there and his work went pleasantly on." Through such conferences the people derived comfort and courage. More than one early church took root in similar fashion, under the leadership of men like Patterson.

Frequently before a frontier family could reach the nearest fort, before they could even leave their cabin, they were caught. Torture was common, although sudden death from a tomahawk blow was more so. Captivity took hundreds of border men, women, and children. Some did not survive captivity; others returned after months or years either through treaty or escape. Many children refused to return to their homes, so little did they remember them and so firmly had they grown into Indian ways.

Captivity was a cruel experience, even for those who were received into the tribes. The rapid marches through wilderness forests; the prospect of death; the sight of one's fellows, one's wife or husband or children, tomahawked or tortured before one's eyes was so appalling that those who survived often lost their minds.

During the years when the Indians were making war the settlers enjoyed little peace except in winter, when Indians were least able to make their invasions into the settlements. Having spent many summer days cooped up in uncomfortable forts, the settlers hailed the approach of winter with joy, for then they could remain in their cabins, which, drafty and smoky as they might be and empty of the most ordinary comforts known to us, were nevertheless home to the border men and women. If their corn had been left to ripen by the Indians and the potatoes had flourished, there was happy activity in gathering and shelling corn, in potato digging, and in repairing the farm tools and cabin for spring. The first frost and the first snow flurry were really welcome, for they were like a lock on the country to fasten it safely from marauding savages.

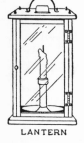

LANTERN

Then when the long, safe winter first promised to break into spring, along toward the last week of February, or early in March, the frontiersman and frontier woman again became doubtful, restive, and expectant. They went about their work with eyes and ears constantly alert for danger. For these first spring thaws that began to open up the frozen lands were the "powwowing days" that preceded the first Indian raids.

In the advancing pageant of migration there occurred more than one dramatic retreat, when large numbers of settlers scooped their goods together and swarmed back toward the mountains and beyond them, where for a time they could rest in safety from Indians harrying the settlements throughout the western end of the state.

The summer of 1774, the time of Dunmore's War, was a remarkable one in this respect. The region west of the Monongahela River was overrun by scalping parties marking their way with blood and destruction. A number of forts, even in the most remote sections, were attacked about the same time. The southwestern section of the state was under a rain of bullets and fire arrows. Panic seized the settlers, and the contagion of terror spread like a forest fire. From almost every cabin, from log fort after log fort, from villages and towns fled men and women and children. They converged from every path upon the roads leading east. Cabins stood open-doored after the hasty departure of their occupants, tables were left set, irons and pots stood on the hearth, and the coverlets from the beds were used to wrap small treasures that could be snatched up. Past their ripening cornfields and flax patches, past the greening cabbage beds and turnips rows, families fled toward the nearest fort, hoping to reach it by nightfall as a stage in their flight. Thronging together at the Monongahela, more than a thousand people crossed in one day at three ferries not one mile apart.

St. Clair, in a letter, told Governor Penn of his observations along the Forbes Road near Fort Ligonier. "I am certain I did not meet less than a hundred Families and I think two Thousand head of cattle in twenty miles riding. . . . yesterday they all moved into this place [*Ligonier*]." Washington's land agent also wrote, "If we had not had forts built there would not have been ten families left this side of the mountains besides what are at Fort Pitt."

But the danger passed for the moment. Gradually the settlers regained their courage. One after another of the families moved back, and new ones came on. The frontiersmen once more took up the work of settlement, although the forts were still necessary and were frequently used from time to time, until finally in 1794 Anthony Wayne's victory at Fallen Timbers, in the Northwest Territory, removed the Indian menace from western Pennsylvania.

Yarbs, Doctors, and Charms

XI

THE rugged, out-of-door life and simple diet of the early western Pennsylvania settlers might, to our modern view, be considered a perfect prescription for good health. But this mode of living was not an unmixed blessing. Their knowledge of hygiene and of the prevention and cure of disease was very limited. What they did know of these things was more through instinct than science. They were subject to the effects of exposure. A settler returning from the winter woods to his cabin, wet, tired, and hungry, would sit before the fire to dry his clothes or lie down to sleep in his clothes, wet as they were, so long as his feet were stretched close to the fire. Warm underwear was almost unknown, and waterproof jackets and heavy overcoats were extremely rare. The unbalanced nature of a diet consisting mainly of corn and meat showed its effects in the jaundiced and pasty complexions of most of the pioneers. No dentists were available to care for their teeth. Illness and physical ailments were considered natural and inescapable and generally the settlers could see no reason for quarantine. The records of Yohogania County, however, reveal "that inhabitants of this county have leave to In-

noculate for the Small pox at their houses or such other convenient Places as they may think proper." In cold weather the
sick and the well slept in the same almost air-tight rooms. Many
diseases were bred by the lack of sanitation, and various fevers
carried off men and women in their prime and rapidly filled
the newly laid out graveyards. Many children died at birth or
in the first year or two of their lives; only the fittest and luckiest
won through. In view of such conditions of ignorance and care-
lessness, it is remarkable that the settlers even survived, let
alone accomplished what they did.

The ague, known also as the "ager" and the "shakes," was
so common that it excited no great concern. People merely
said, "He's not sick; he's just got the ager." The sufferer endured his symptoms as best he could—yawnings and stretch-
ings, weakness and lack of energy, sweating, and cold chills
that increased until his teeth chattered uncontrollably. With
returning warmth came raging fever, with pains racking his
head and back. A spell of ague might last for weeks, chills and
fever coming close together or alternating one day with another. Schedules of work, of courting, and of business were
arranged in accordance with the regular attacks. Cholera and
typhoid epidemics came and went with the seasons. Knowing
how unsanitary were the conditions of that day, we suspect that
most of their fevers were typhoid. The pioneers believed that
these diseases were caused by night air, decaying refuse, unripe
fruit, lack of sleep, grief, and worry. Contagious diseases such
as scarlet fever, measles, mumps, and chicken pox were considered unavoidable and necessary steps in the development
to adulthood. Children in good health were often deliberately

exposed to the milder diseases in order to get the sickness "over with." Erysipelas and skin disorders spread through communities. Pneumonia, or "lung fever," was common and nearly everyone suffered from rheumatism.

The means for fighting these diseases were tragic in their inadequacy. Treatment was largely domestic and primitive, and often superstitious and unsound. Not until the resources of home remedies and theories had been exhausted was the doctor called, if indeed there was one within calling distance. The country doctor, willing and eager to help as he might be, was limited in many ways. He frequently struggled through uncut forests and battled with swollen streams to reach his patients. A branch overhead or a hole underfoot might throw MORTAR him from his horse. When he at last arrived, his lore was per- AND PESTLE haps insufficient. His training had been obtained not in a medical college but as the apprentice of another doctor, whose horse he had cared for and whose pills, as large as cherries, he had rolled while he gathered what scraps of information he could until he was ready to begin his own practice.

He placed his greatest faith in bloodletting and purgatives and emetics. The treatments he used were often more painful than the wounds and disorders he sought to heal, but they were the only theories he knew. Thus, to relieve an irritation, he sometimes threaded a horse hair through a fold of skin or kept a pea or a bit of lint in an incision. A coil of corded cotton was treated to burn slowly so that when laid on the skin it irritated steadily. To cauterize a wound he seared it with a hot iron. To cure a fever or delirium he first bled the patient until the sufferer was near exhaustion; he gave an emetic of ipecac, a cathartic of calomel, and then opium to quiet the disturbed internal organs. All this time the patient probably lay in a close room and was denied cooling drinks. If he suffered from the dumb ague, which was mostly fever rather than chills, the patient was carried outside, laid uncovered on a piece of sacking, and buckets of cold spring water were poured over him until he had a "decided and pretty powerful smart chance of a shake." It is amazing that anyone withstood such drastic though well-intentioned teatment.

SASSAFRAS

The frontiersman relied on herbs and superstition for his home cures. Almost all childish ailments were ascribed to worms, for which the child was given scrapings from pewter spoons and large doses of "pink and senna" or sugar and turpentine. For older people all sorts of remedies were used. The local "yarb and root doctor" (in nearly every community there was some one considered skilled in the care of the sick and the use of herbs) prescribed for fevers such remedies as snakeroot, sassafras, dogwood, willow, white walnut bark peeled upward, or a glass of pearlash and water. If no one was at hand to supervise the bloodletting, pleurisy was treated with catnip and pennyroyal, butterfly weed tea, or brimstone, sulphur, and eggs. For burns, what might seem to be the remains of an average dinner was used in poultices of scraped potatoes, toasted turnips, and corn meal with slippery elm bark.

Snakebite was dealt with externally through cupping, that is, drawing the blood to the surface by means of a vacuum, and covering an incision around the bite with salt and gunpowder; for internal treatment the patient drank "Monongahela rye" or a beverage of plantain in boiled milk. A gunshot wound was treated with slippery elm bark. The "itch" sent the early pioneer to two basic materials, brimstone and hog's lard, which were mixed into an ointment and applied to the affected area. Materials at hand were used for various purposes: grease from the Christmas goose was good for sore throat; a poultice of scraped potatoes was supposed to cure headache; cancer was believed to be cured by a poultice of a teaspoonful of scrapings from a brass kettle mixed with mutton suet. For rheumatism, oils from rattlesnakes, geese, wolves, bears, raccoons, ground hogs, and even skunks were applied to the painful areas. Common coughs and lung disorders were treated with syrups, usually of spikenard and elecampane.

Strange things were done by the pioneers in their attempts to ease the sufferings endured by those they loved. At many of their practices we smile, but the people who in their ignorance employed such cures did so with the utmost faith. To prevent bedsores (when a patient was bedfast), a crock or an ax was put under the bed. In case of kidney trouble, for which there was no careful diagnosis, goat urine was given. One remedy for the ague was to hang a spider around the neck of the sufferer. To cure epilepsy the heart of a rattlesnake was eaten, or a forked hickory tree was split open and the halves wedged apart at the crotch, the victim was passed through three times, and the wedge removed; if the tree healed and grew the patient would recover. Erysipelas was cause for any black cat in the neighborhood to run, for the pioneers believed that the blood of a black cat could cure this disease. The result was that scarcely one in the neighborhood could be found without at least a piece of its ear missing. They also wrapped an eel skin about a sprain, tied a toad to a snake bite to draw out the poison, and thought bed-wetting could be cured by spanking with a bake-oven mop or by having the child eat fried mouse pie.

Certainly the early settlers waged a valiant struggle against adversity, intensified not only by the constant threat and reality of illness, but even by the dangers of their so-called cures and remedies.

Settlers who were cut off from doctors who might have explained their illnesses, or from intelligent neighbors who could have told them why a crop had failed, often gave strange reasons for such things. Poorly informed, without books or printed guides, some individuals of all racial elements fell back on superstitious explanations that primitive peoples had used for centuries. It was easier to explain the sudden death of the single cow that supplied a family with milk or the strange behavior of a watchdog by blaming such occurrences on witches and spells rather than to find the real reason. Many defenseless women who were perhaps queer or merely aged were accused of witchcraft simply because they lived near families who suffered misfortune. When a mishap coincided with the passing by of such a woman from up the branch or along the ridge, the two events were related in the mind of the untaught settler. The conclusion reached was that the woman must be a witch. Old tales of witchcraft were revived by those who had heard such tales in their childhood in Europe.

It was believed that animals, children, and objects could be *verhext,* or bewitched, in a number of ways. Persons with such power were said to destroy cattle by shooting them with hair balls. They were also accused of putting spells on guns that missed their mark, on knives and tools that were mislaid. They were said to have changed men into horses that they bridled, saddled, and rode furiously over the hills to their witches' Sabbaths or meetings. Many a pioneer believed his cow had gone dry because a witch had milked her. This the witch was supposed to do by fastening a new pin in a new towel for each cow to be milked. The towels she then hung over her doorway, and, as she repeated her incantations, she drew milk from the fringe of the towels after the manner of milking the cows. Cattle and dogs believed to be bewitched were burned on the forehead with a branding iron. If an animal died under the spell of a witch its whole body was burned to ashes. A witch could inflict strange and incurable diseases, such as dropsy of the brain or rickets. For rickets, or "falling away," the German settlers had a strange cure. At sundown the child so inflicted was measured with a piece of red string. If the length of the body as measured by the string was less than seven times the length of the child's foot, the string was made into a loop and the child was passed through it three times while a charm was repeated. The string was then tied round a grindstone. When the string had worn out the child would have attained its proper length.

Charms spoken to effect such cures were treasured in secrecy. Such charms might be told by a man to a woman or by a woman to a man. But if told by a woman to a woman or by a man to a man they lost their magic. Knowledge of such charms brought down upon women who knew them the charge of being a witch; men who could use them were looked upon as wizards.

But the power of a witch could be broken, the pioneers believed, and they had several devices for this purpose. If a crudely superstitious family believed an illness to be the result of "verhexing," they drew on a board or a log the picture of a witch. This they shot at with a bullet containing a bit of silver. Such a bullet was supposed to transfer the spell from the patient to the witch. If the bullet struck the arm of the drawing the witch's arm became affected; if it struck her thigh in the drawing, the spell was transferred to her thigh.

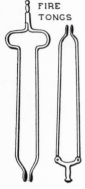

FIRE
TONGS

A witch could in turn break the spell she was put under. To do this she borrowed some object from the family that had put the spell on her. Frequently an innocent old woman who had many times borrowed a pan or an iron from a neighbor was puzzled one day to find her request refused and was heartbroken when she learned the reason for refusal.

The fertility of more than one frontier farm was thought to be helped more by charms and "powwowing" than by fertilizing and rotating crops. Ignorant farmers preferred to consult almanacs for the signs of heavenly bodies rather than actual weather signs to decide whether or not to do their planting. By the "waxing and waning" of the moon, as indicated in his almanac, such a farmer sowed his grain or butchered his meat so that it would not shrink in the pot. He planted his vegetables when the sun was in the correct relation to the zodiacal sign of Virgo so that they would not run to seed. All this he did not understand, but he followed faithfully the directions in his almanac calendar. If crops were withering from drought, it was believed that crouching on the ground and clapping two stones together while a charm was repeated would bring rain. Boys whistled while tapping green bark as they made willow whistles in spring. This, too, was a charm for rain. They did not know that primitive people had done the same thing long ages ago because the water spirit was supposed to live in willows along a stream.

Rats became numerous in this grain-growing region. Spells were put on them for riddance, particularly by the Germans, whose customs and superstitions have been more frequently preserved in writing than those of the other groups of early settlers. A note was written to the rats charging them to vacate the premises, just as it would have been written to any other tenant, and new quarters were suggested for them at a neighbor's farm. The notice was folded and pushed into a rat hole, where it was gnawed to pieces as acknowledgment of receipt. On the next moonlight night, it was asserted, the careful observer could see the rats marching in a long line to the new home assigned to them.

Belief was strong, too, in the good or bad influence of certain days of the year. A sick woman would not get up on a Sunday lest she should never get well. Friday was also an unfortunate day. On Ascension Day the housewife must not sweep her cabin lest it become infested with fleas. To finish a piece of spinning, weaving, or sewing, she would sit up late at night so that it need not be finished on that holy day. A nameless German settler is quoted as saying, "My mother knew a girl who sewed on Ascension Day, and there came a gust and killed her." Christmas, Easter, and New Year's each had its superstitions. A child born on Christmas night had power to see supernatural sights and to hear sounds no other mortal could hear and at the stroke of twelve on Christmas eve could hear all the animals talking together. In some sections the custom of "firing in" the new year was observed: young people went from cabin to cabin, stood around the door, called greetings and good wishes in rhymes, and fired off their guns for good luck. At Easter it was thought a rabbit would lay eggs if a bonnet was put out as a nest. Colored flowers were gathered and left for the Easter rabbit to eat so that the eggs would be colored ones.

Allhallows eve, or as we know it, Halloween, was a time when young girls, eager to see their future husband, took a looking-glass in hand and walked downstairs backward, or climbed down the ladder from the loft, to catch his reflection in the glass. Or they melted lead and poured it into a cup of cold water to discover in the shapes it took some indication of his trade—a soldier's cap, a book, or a horse. After locks and keys came into use, the melted lead was poured through the hole in the handle of the door key. St. Andrew's night, the thirtieth of November, was also a night for this practice. After the pouring of lead, the girls filled their mouths with water so that they would not talk, for talking broke the spell. Such charms were survivals of days when all metal was thought to have magic power. Among the Germans, the young women also observed the custom of eating salt cake, then going to bed backward without speaking or drinking, and in their dreams that night would be revealed the future husband. As marriage was more of a necessity on the frontier than in settled regions, young women used many such charms in their eagerness to know into what young man's hands their fates would fall. They walked around the cabin or house and listened for the first man's name they should overhear, for it belonged to him who would ask them in marriage. Two girls together tied a key between the pages of the Bible so that the handle protruded; then each held the handle by a finger tip and one of them repeated a charm, each line of which began with a different letter. At the initial of the future husband of the girl repeating the charm, the key and the Bible turned slightly.

Often frontier matches were made between a woman and a man of unequal age or of unequal standing in the settlement. Then a group gathered about the cabin of the couple, and with pans, guns, sticks, and other instruments made *Katzen-musik,* or "cat music," as a grotesque serenade.

By all these devices, and by many others, frontier people tried to draw around them the protective powers of good luck and to ward off evil fortune. A way of life in which help was often far distant and in which danger came quickly made people desperate to employ any means they could for safety and happiness. Practices long forgotten, long lost in their child-hood, and first learned in the childhood of the world were revived as immediate help in time of trouble.

The Log Church

XII

THE first Christian religious services in the western Pennsylvania wilderness, so far as our records show, were the Roman Catholic mass and prayers said by Fathers Vernet and Queret, who accompanied the Baron de Longueuil on his expedition into the region in 1739, and those said by the Jesuit Father Bonnecamps a decade later, when Céloron's royal expedition floated down the Allegheny River. In 1754, shortly after the French had captured and re-christened Fort Duquesne, the Recollet Father Denys Baron celebrated mass on the site of Pittsburgh and dedicated a chapel to "The Assumption of the Blessed Virgin of the Beautiful River." Here, until the fort was abandoned four years later, he and his successors devoted themselves to the spiritual and physical welfare of their flock, baptizing the children of the French settlers, binding the wounds of the English captives, and teaching the word of life to the painted warriors gathered in the bark village outside the fort.

On Christmas Day, 1750, Christopher Gist had read the Christmas service of the Protestant Episcopal Church to the Indians at Coshocton, Ohio. Four years later Colonel George

Washington read public prayers at Fort Necessity, and the next year, in place of the regular chaplain, who had been severely wounded, he read the burial service over General Braddock at Great Meadows. The Reverend Charles Beatty, a Presbyterian, traveled with the army of General John Forbes in 1758, and late in November of that year he preached the first Protestant sermon on the site of the future Pittsburgh. For the next few years religious services were held occasionally by chaplains and missionaries at Pittsburgh as well as at other forts in the region.

In these early years, however, there were continuous religious services for the settlers of western Pennsylvania. The cabin hearth, its flames casting a ruddy glow upon the bowed heads of the family, was the first altar, and here the pioneer father and mother heard their children repeat their prayers and told stories of Abraham and Isaac and of the star of Bethlehem. Before itinerant—that is, traveling—ministers threaded the trails, and before the log churches were filled with the singing of psalms, the first principles of religion, like the first steps in education, were taught at the family hearth. Although children were brought up without having been baptized, they were taught their A B C's and the fear of God from the pioneer Bible, frequently the only book owned, its pages crumpled and smudged from rains soaking through the logs and from grimy fingers following the lines by the light of the fire and the smoking tallow dip.

So eager were the settlers to establish religious worship, both in their desire for communion with God and in their longing for fellowship, that they took advantage of whatever occasions and places offered, sometimes within a fort or stockade, sometimes in a neighbor's cabin, sometimes under the open sky.

Presbyterians adopted the custom of gathering together in their cabins in "praying societies." These groups were at first composed of the families that had migrated together and had settled near one another; then of the families that, migrating alone, had soon made friends with their neighbors. At these meetings a man who had been an elder of his church in the East would read from the Bible by the light of a smoking pine knot or tallow dip and would lead in prayer and in the singing of solemn old psalms or hymns. Later the settlers gathered together and raised cabins to serve as both church and school. In these, the bare ground was usually the floor, there were seldom any heating devices, and the congregation sat on log benches. The churches eventually were built in more permanent form, with rough stone foundations, but they were not always large enough for the crowds that gathered for Communion services. At such times the groves were God's temples. A stump or a slab log fastened between two trees served as the pulpit, and logs took the place of pews. A platform, or "tent," as it was called, was erected to protect the ministers, and the congregation, like the Galileans, sat on the hillside around. The broad faces of halved logs served as Communion tables.

Early German settlers followed much the same procedure as the Presbyterians. Their informal meetings were, however, more cheerful. One of the settlers might possess a book of sermons by an early church father, from which, or from the Bible, passages were read. A man who was asked why churches were built before a preacher had settled among them replied that one of the chief reasons for going to church was that they liked to "listen to Barbara Brandenburg sing." As help from the East was slow in coming to the Germans, certain of their people took upon themselves more and more of the ministerial duties. There were instances where those not qualified to do so conducted the marriage service.

The earliest Methodist settlers in western Pennsylvania listened to the preaching and spiritual counsel of a fervent member of their group until an itinerant preacher happened to pass through their community. The Methodist doctrine was new in America at the time these settlers were moving into western Pennsylvania, but after 1784 itinerant preachers were regularly assigned to circuits in the region. Because such preachers served a very large territory, Methodists even then had to content themselves with class meetings for long periods. Bishop Francis Asbury, founder of the Methodist Church in America, himself visited the region sixteen times during the pioneer period.

Missionaries of the Baptist denomination sometimes traveled through the district. The Baptist Church did not require that its ministers be educated men and often permitted a "gifted brother" to preach. Thus a group of Baptists might begin to hold services among themselves immediately upon their arrival in the western country.

Quakers found services easier than any of the other sects. Wherever two or three were "gathered together in God's name" a Quaker meeting could be held.

The Episcopalian Church, to which many settlers of English descent might have been drawn, had been weakened by strug-

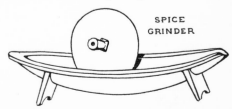

SPICE
GRINDER

gles in the East, where, as a Tory church, it had met strong opposition. Its service was perhaps too elaborate for the simplicity of pioneer tastes, and its vestments, altar services, and music did not lend themselves readily to the random occasions when church services were possible. It could consequently do little for frontier people and could not follow up what little it managed to accomplish. Prominent Episcopalians, however, did their best to remedy this situation. Thus, General John Neville built a church at Woodville, served in it as a lay reader, and financed the education of its first minister.

Many early settlers of western Pennsylvania, to be sure, had left their old homes to be free from the regulations and restraints imposed on them. Many were glad that the seat of government was far away, and they would have been equally happy not to have churches near to try to make them lead more orderly lives. Most settlers, however, had given up their old churches with heavy hearts and were eager to get new ones started as soon as possible. Those interested in prosperous farms and new industries, moreover, realized that the founding of churches would encourage progress. The government realized, too, that with the development of churches better order would prevail in the communities and it would be called upon less often to take a hand.

In the East, church members and church governing bodies looked upon the frontier region with pity, and, imbued with the missionary spirit, sent out missionaries to preach to both Indians and whites. Almost every year for more than a decade after 1763, the Presbyterian synod of New York and Philadelphia made an effort to see that sermons were preached and that marriage and baptismal services were held in the wilderness beyond the mountains. Although Indian troubles made extended journeys dangerous, several ministers made important trips. On horseback from Carlisle came Charles Beatty and George Duffield in 1766. James Finley, who later settled in western Pennsylvania, came out in 1771.

From New England, in 1772, two newly ordained Congregationalists, David McClure and Levi Frisbie, journeyed into the region to convert the Indians and to preach to white settlers as occasion offered. Some of these settlers, McClure said, had not heard a sermon for fourteen years. His diary gives a good idea of the state of religious feeling and education in the country through which he traveled. It gives also many sidelights on the social habits and customs. He found that the majority of the people made the Sabbath a day of recreation and drinking. At the time there was no settled minister or church organization west of the Appalachians. "The people are generally presbyterians. A few illiterate preachers of the baptist persuasion, have preached about, zealous to make proselytes." Frisbie and McClure reached the Muskingum country but, dissatisfied with their work among the Indians, they returned to the Pittsburgh district. McClure said:

"The inhabitants of this place are very dissipated. They seem to feel themselves beyond the arm of government, & freed from the restraining influence of religion. It is the resort of Indian traders, & many here have escaped from Justice & from Creditors, in the old settlements. . . . We found, however, a happy few who live in the fear of God, & maintain their integrity."

In the Ligonier country McClure found five new settlements, in all of which he was asked to stay and preach. He felt that his services were needed and consented to stay until the following May or June, during which time he devoted his time in succession to the settlements in that district. "It was pleasing to find in each of them, some zealous and pious persons, who came forward, & willingly devoted their time & labours to form the people into a society, for the purpose of the public worship of God." He also found a settlement of Virginians, quite different from the Presbyterians and Germans, and "much addicted to drinking parties, gambling, horse race & fighting."

Two of the most important early missionaries were the Reverend James Power, who made a tour in 1774 and a few years later settled in the frontier region, and the Reverend John McMillan, who came out in 1776. These two energetic individuals, both Presbyterians, gave many of the early settlers in western Pennsylvania the first taste of formal religion they had had since they had left their old homes.

As settlement expanded, order and stability came to characterize the churches. The Presbyterian praying societies sent requests eastward for preachers, and their entreaties brought response. Four Presbyterian ministers, all of them men of ability and character, settled in the region between 1776 and 1780. These four—John McMillan, James Power, Thaddeus Dodd, and Joseph Smith—each had two or more congregations in his charge and in addition made long preaching tours into remote sections where preachers had not yet settled. Within the next few years four other ministers joined them. So great became the demand that the East could not find men to fill the western pulpits.

Three of the early preachers, therefore, decided to keep their eyes open for likely young men whom they could train as ministers without lowering the standards under which they themselves had been trained in the East. About 1782 Dodd's neighbors built him a cabin in which to conduct a school. Joseph Smith also opened a school. Most important, however, was the log school opened by Dr. McMillan, which became, in 1791, the Canonsburg Academy and which in 1792 was approved by the Redstone Presbytery as its official training school for its ministers.

MAPLE

As early as 1787 a group of German Catholics had settled at Sportsman's Hall, now St. Vincent's, in Westmoreland County, and a few years later a number of these settlers went on to found a Catholic colony near Waynesburg. In 1775 a number of Irish Catholics settled on what was later the line between Butler and Armstrong counties, and about 1805 men of the neighborhood gathered and built in one day the log chapel known as St. Patrick's Sugar Creek Church. The log building may still be seen standing adjacent to the more modern structure now in use as a church home. In 1790 a settlement was begun by Captain Michael McGuire in what is now Cambria County on the site of Loretto. Other Catholic settlers came in the following years and in 1799 Father Demetrius Gallitzin joined them as their spiritual guide.

Father Gallitzin was born a Russian prince in 1770. He came to Baltimore in 1792 and three years later became the second priest ordained in the United States. At Loretto he invested his fortune in aiding Catholic settlers to obtain homes in the vicinity, and his latter years were burdened by the debts that he incurred in this endeavor. His first chapel was completed by Christmas, 1799, and in this log building and its successors he ministered until his death in 1840. He always insisted upon strict propriety in the chapel and he hung in the vestibule the following rules:

    I Scrape the dirt off your shoes on the iron scrapers provided for that purpose.
    II Do not spit on the floor of the chapel.
    III Do not put your hats and caps on the chapel windows.
    IV Do not rub against the papered walls of the chapel.
    V Do not put your heels on the washboards.
    VI After coming in at the passage door shut the door after you.

The stone chapel of 1832 has been restored in recent years. It contains Father Gallitzin's original altar, encased in stone and flanked by wood carvings from Oberammergau. The windows are of stained glass, one of them set with the Gallitzin arms, and in the belfry above is the bell first used in the region to call the devout to worship. Father Gallitzin lived in two rooms adjoining the chapel, now one apartment containing relics connected with his life. His tomb and statue may be seen in the churchyard near by.

As Catholic settlements spread beyond Loretto Father Gallitzin gave more and more of his time to visiting other preaching points and ministering to isolated parishioners. In his old age he traveled on a horse-drawn sled even in the summer, for the roads were too primitive to accommodate a wheeled vehicle. The region is full of reminders of Father Gallitzin's ministry:

here is the long steep road up which he labored and the gratefully cool spring whose limpid current he blessed; and here
in a cabin above the fireplace is the mantelpiece on which he
placed the chalice while he stood before the worshippers kneel-
ing on the cabin floor and said the mass.

Through the combined efforts of the people on the frontier
who wanted churches and of the people back home who
thought they should have them, churches were gradually established in western Pennsylvania. This does not mean that every
individual in a community where there was a church belonged
to it nor that every district where there were settlers had one
or more churches. In fact, it is probable that not more than
one-sixth of the entire population of western Pennsylvania
during the pioneer period were church members. It is true,
nevertheless, that churches were sufficiently numerous and
sufficiently strong to dominate completely many parts of the
region and to exercise an influence for progress and for good
in the region as a whole.

Among Presbyterians Sunday began with family worship in
the cabin. Then the father in his best jeans and the mother in
her best linsey, with their children often barefoot and the
youngest carried in their arms, walked or rode horseback to
the nearest log church. At ten o'clock in the morning, huddled
in the dim, crowded room, the congregation droned the long
hymns. A leader "lined out" the hymns, singing one line at
a time, which the congregation repeated after him. Long
prayers were offered, during which the children were apt to
grow restless. Very long sermons were preached, most frequently on eternal punishment and the horrors of hell. The

air in the room grew hot and stuffy. Faces perspired; backs ached; the log seats grew more uncomfortable. Children whimpered and were roughly quieted. Eyelids drooped and heads nodded. The preacher became vehement to stifle the yawns and to jerk up the drooping shoulders. After several hours of such service the congregation took a recess. Baskets and kerchiefs in which lunches had been packed were opened. If the weather was fine, the contents were spread outside on the grass or a stump. After such brief recess the little crowd again ranged themselves on the hard log seats for the afternoon service. Now the lined-out psalms seemed endless; the long prayers rose and fell to the accompaniment of shiftings of feet and of arms that ached from the burden of sleeping babies. To relieve cramped muscles and to fight off drowsiness members would stand or even pace back and forth along the sides or backs of the pews.

Communion was a solemn occasion. Since only ordained ministers could administer it, in the early period it was neither frequent nor regular. Among the Presbyterians the Thursday preceding this service was observed as a fast day or day of prayer and rest from labor. As congregations frequently combined for Communion, the houses of those who lived near the church overflowed with visitors for the several days of the season. On Saturday services were held "to fix the truths." Those members in good standing were given tokens or bits of inscribed lead, which entitled them to Communion on the Sunday. Since meetinghouses were too small for the crowds, services were held in the groves, although in rainy weather, barns, when available, were used. At least two ministers, frequently three or four, administered the service. After hymns, prayers, and the first sermon, "fencing the tables" took up an hour or more. This was a review of all the sins forbidden in the ten commandments. Those guilty of any sin were excluded. Then a welcome to Communion was preached. The tables were filled six or seven times before all were accommodated. The Monday following was a day of great celebration.

Among Methodists, quarterly meetings, at which Communion was administered, supplied a socializing influence. From miles around, preachers, elders, class leaders, and congregations assembled in groves. Houses and cabins were crowded with praying, singing, and visiting families eager to feel in common those emotions that lay so deep and that held them in common brotherhood. The Methodist hymns, spirited and martial, swinging along in evangelical refrains, rocked in rhythm whole groves of assembled worshippers and gave vent to feelings long pent up through lack of community life. Fervid, almost rollicking, these tunes carried themes of salvation sought and achieved. The leaves of the trees must have trembled at hundreds of voices shouting triumphant redemption.

It is not strange that frontier people, denied close and constant neighborliness, often let their feelings break out, when the opportunity offered, in violent expressions. Their games and dancing, their political discussions, their friendships, and their revenge for injustice, all were expressed with much greater vehemence than by people who are day by day in touch with their fellows and who, therefore, are constantly expressing their normal feelings, their little pleasures and discontents. In their religious hopes and fears the frontier people were no different than in their amusements, their politics, and their

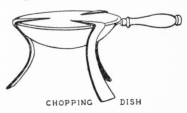

CHOPPING DISH

neighborhood relationships. They were repressed for months at a time. Bad weather and roads, not to mention lack of shoes and suitable clothing, made it difficult to gather and to praise God for his care and protection, to ease conscience by confession or testimony, and to seek comfort and help from stronger characters.

When they did meet, their feelings broke out in great joy and relief or in fearful self-accusation. These were the times when revivals of religious life took place. Communion services often brought on these revivals, when several preachers assisted one another. At their joint preachings, their threats of burning punishments, and promises of heavenly happiness, many in the congregation bowed their heads in prayer and some cried out in anguish of soul. The pious shouted and clapped their hands, swayed in their seats and cried out "Amen!" In 1795 McMillan's congregation at Chartiers experienced such a revival; fifty members were added to his church, some of whom later became ministers. Four years later another revival brought sixty more into the fold. Frequently there was backsliding, indifference, and great discouragement on the part of those who had previously been so wrought up, until they were once more reminded.

Revivals were often held as camp meetings, lasting a number of days. Services sometimes continued all night long, minister following minister, while listeners came and went, weeping and rejoicing loudly, shouting praises, and falling on the ground in anguished repentance. "Falling work" and "bodily exercises" held many in trances, prone on the ground, unable to move for hours. In the Great Revival, which in 1802 swept through Kentucky, Tennessee, the Carolinas, West Virginia, and western Pennsylvania, this falling work was particularly prevalent. At one of the meetings, in spite of snow and rain, families came in wagons from miles away and camped. Nine ministers preached, frequently two of them at once. There were eight hundred communicants. This was in September. In November another service was held, at which fifteen ministers were present. It is said ten thousand gathered in wagons, bringing food and bedding. The Reverend Elisha Macurdy preached the most famous sermon of his career. At his words many fell to the ground.

Released from the excitement of revivals, the frontier communities settled back into everyday life. People had to rely then on the more ordinary comfort and help of their own consciences. For support in their daily difficulties they depended on the reading of the Bible and on the regular Church services or, in less fortunate communities, on the infrequent visits of a traveling preacher. In communities that did not have a regular pastor, word was sent ahead of the coming of a traveling preacher and the scattered settlements looked forward with eagerness to another occasion for gathering. The devout were glad of the chance to hear the sermon. The others were glad of the opportunity to exchange news and the gossip of the section. Ministers rarely disappointed their flocks. The faithfulness of the early itinerant Methodist passed into a proverb: on stormy days people said the weather was so bad that nothing was out but crows and Methodist preachers.

When a ministerial call was expected by a family, mother and children swept and garnished, scoured and baked, and prepared the wild turkey that father had shot in the woods. The most important man in the community was paying a visit. The elders around the hearth would be sure of a sympathetic listener to their trials and daily sorrows; they were sure of a strengthening word and a helpful prayer for their individual grace. And the children would come in for their share of attention when they were asked to stand up and recite verses from Scripture and to show how they were learning to read the story of the boy Jesus in the temple, or if they were Presbyterians they were tested for memorizing passages from the catechism.

Growth of churches brought growth of orderliness to the frontier. Since settlers were remote from courts and police officers, the discipline that the church exercised over the lives of its members was a great force for decency and order. The Methodists had their book of discipline, revised by the Methodist General Conference and enforced locally by the preachers. Quaker rules of conduct were enforced by committees of Friends, which supervised cases of discipline. The Baptists drew up covenants to watch over one another's lives and conversation and not to "suffer sin upon each other but encourage one another to love and good works." A German congregation drew up the following specifications for personal conduct among their members:

"Who ever shall work on Sundays or on the festal days, if such is unnecessary and not a work of love, or gets drunk, dances or gambles or allows any sinful or wicked company in his house, or is present any time when the name of God is insulted or profaned and thus cause trouble in the congregation,

BOOT
JACKS

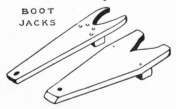

and brings many innocent souls into sin and punishment, shall for the first offense be brought before the preacher and consistory."

A church could not jail its members or deprive them of any recognized civic privileges. It enforced its control by appealing to the natural desire of human beings for the good will of their community and by depriving them of church privileges. First offenders got off with a scolding or a warning. If the offender acknowledged his guilt and made a statement of repentance he lost no standing. Frequently the facts of misbehavior were "published" in the congregation to humiliate the offender and to prevent the spreading of the particular misbehavior. One man was obliged to make public apology for having struck his wife. A man in the Dunlaps Creek congregation was not allowed to have his children baptized because he used "unguarded expressions" at times. When he acknowledged his guilt, professed his sorrow, and promised to be on his guard in the future, the baptism of his children was performed. The Quakers, who were most severe, "disowned" offenders; that is, removed them from church rolls. Other denominations used the same punishment for the worst transgressors.

The Sabbath was fanatically observed among Presbyterians. Not even traveling or visiting was allowed. Two brothers who drove home their teams from some distance away were tried by the church for the offense. A man who allowed his son to make sugar on the Sabbath was called up by the congregation. The postmaster at Washington was not allowed to open the mails on Sunday, although such business was legal.

The church also kept strict watch over week-day activities.

Attending horse races, frequenting inns for card playing and cockfighting, dancing in public, and watching bear baiting were forbidden. Men and women were brought before their congregations for quarreling, for speaking rashly, and for talking scandalously about even their neighbors' children. Persons were suspended from churches for lying.

Churches often handled cases that a justice of the peace might have been expected to handle. The Westland Quakers "disowned" two women for "opening the Door of the House when the Family were absent and taking several things out." John Blane, a Presbyterian, was deprived of church privileges until he should show signs of repentance for taking some flour not his own from an adjacent mill. In another church the case came up of a man who sold whiskey "which froze in the bottle," showing that it had been diluted with water, and who received more pay than he should according to agreement.

In some frontier communities virtuous people formed "watch and ward societies," whose aims were to help civil authorities discover and convict those found guilty of vice and immorality and to enforce the observance of the Sabbath. Drinking and gaming, disorderly meetings, profanity, and taking the name of God in vain were mentioned as demanding their particular attention.

Presbyterianism took an early hold on the western Pennsylvania frontier, stronger than any other denomination. On other frontiers the Methodists and Baptists rooted themselves most strongly. Thus the minds of the people were not harassed by confusing appeals; and many were won to Presbyterian doctrine, to its morality and guidance in everyday living. Perhaps it tightened life a little too much, restricted or forbade community and personal pleasures that would have eased the rough road of the pioneers. But it was in the long run a beneficent social agency. It focused and made concrete by church doctrine and practice many general ideals by which early settlers tried to live.

CANDLE STICK

Frontier Justice

XIII

IN THE process of settlement it was not long until the
frontier family had to learn to live not as a self-sufficing
farm community but with neighbors in a much more complex community life. Concern of the individual for his own
safety and welfare and for those of his family broadened with
advancing settlement to concern for the safety and welfare of
larger groups—the neighborhood, the church, and the school—
and for the administration of justice in county and township.

A frontier code of living developed, one that the pioneer
himself followed and that he forced on his fellows; it was an
unwritten code but it was effective until counties and town-
ships were legally set up, until officers such as constables and
justices of the peace were appointed, and until churches and
law courts developed. While population was sparse and while
settlers were threatened by war and other dangers, public
opinion was effective, and in public opinion were found the
first principles of justice by which frontiersmen lived. Old
sayings and saws were quoted and lived by as town ordinances
might have been. "Honesty is the best policy" and similar sayings were brought forth on suitable occasions as warnings or

rebukes. Rights were defended and punishment for invading the rights of others was administered by the settlers themselves. The rough-and-tumble of frontier life promoted democracy. The church and the law were for many years far on the other side of the mountains, so that their influences were slow in reaching the frontier. Thus the community itself was obliged in times of peril to choose its leaders, and authority was given to any one who proved himself capable, without regard to how much land he owned, how large was his cabin or drove of cattle, where he had come from, or who his ancestors had been. Men and women who held lands and homes at the price of bloodshed were not going to play with right and justice; they were in deadly earnest. A false decision might break up the organization of the feeble community life. Since they could not always afford to wait for the advice of a government whose seat was some days' journey across the mountains, these early communities acted in most instances as small independent states.

Many acts considered on the frontier as socially injurious crimes demanding correction would pass unnoticed today in our more highly organized community life. Lying, idleness, and dishonesty were serious crimes because they interfered with the work of settlement. Those who refused to do their share in house-raising or harvesting or who indulged in thievery, lying, or slander interfered with the simple routine of life. To accuse a man of such misconduct was to invite a fight, for it branded a man as an antisocial person in the community, and antisocial persons interfered with the business of defending the fort, endangered property claims, disrupted the community, and caused quarrels when unified action was necessary to carry out a scouting expedition or a campaign.

The common way of handling such offenders was to "hate them out" of the community; that is, to make living so difficult for them that they were forced to leave the neighborhood. Failure to perform his share of military duty caused a man to be hated out as a coward. Failure to accompany a scouting party in his turn placed a man in bad standing with his neighbors. Epithets of dishonor were mercilessly fastened to his name. In cases of theft, groups of settlers might meet together to determine the guilt of the person suspected. They punished him by administering, in true Mosaic fashion, stripes on his back, usually thirteen, but often the Biblical number of "forty less one." Flogging was used also to extort a confession of guilt, a method that at times resulted in more injustice than justice. Confession was often followed by exile. The device of "sweating" was also resorted to. The offender was suspended from the limb of a tree by his arms, and lashes were then "laid on" by several men in turn.

Until counties were erected, enforcement of the written laws of the province, when not effected by public opinion, was in the hands of the military commandant at Fort Pitt. When settlers, for instance, were forbidden to come into the territory after 1763, it was his task to see that they were kept out. He also enforced regulations for the Indian trade. Kenny records in his journal for November, 1761:

"As to ye Government of ye Place [*Pittsburgh*] at present ye Chief Laws have been Out by ye General's Orders, which are Viz 1st That all Subjects may by applying to ye Chief Enginear

Build Houses, but none to Sell or Rent any; that no person shall buy of ye Indians, Horses nor Bells, &c. . . . . To Sell no Rum or Strong Liquor nor give to Indians on Pain of having their Houses pull'd Down & ye Transgressors being banished the place. There was also some time ago, restrictions about Selling the Indians Powdr & Lead to exceed five pounds for one man at Once of Each & that there must be no dealing in Trade after ye Evening Gun is fired after Sun Down."

Not until county boundaries were established could county courts be set up and justices of the province appointed to carry out the law within the counties. If frontiersmen could not settle their disputes either peaceably or by means of a good fight or by force of community opinion, they were compelled to travel over the mountains to Carlisle to seek legal redress for their grievances. With formal courts far distant and roads difficult and dangerous to travel it was little wonder that they often took affairs into their own hands.

The first county to include land west of the Alleghenies was Cumberland County, erected January 27, 1750. Its jurisdiction over southwestern Pennsylvania was established on November 5, 1768, by the treaty with the Six Nations at Fort Stanwix, New York. In 1771 Bedford County was formed from part of Cumberland, and a county seat was established at Bedford, a hundred miles from Pittsburgh. Here, on April 16, 1771, met the first Pennsylvania courts to serve western Pennsylvania settlers in their own territory. They had jurisdiction over the newly established Pitt Township, which included nearly all of the southwestern part of the province. The hardships and dangers of travel that Pittsburghers and farther removed set-

tlers underwent to attend court at Bedford occasioned the erec-
tion, in February, 1773, of a new county, Westmoreland, and
the establishment therein of a new court. Pittsburgh was then
in Westmoreland County, and a dispute arose as to whether
the county seat of the new county should be at Fort Pitt or
at the new settlement of Hannastown, four miles northwest
of Greensburg. One faction was led by General Arthur St.
Clair, who favored Fort Pitt, and the other by Robert Hanna
and Joseph Erwin, who favored Hannastown. Hanna, who
had served as one of the justices at the Bedford court, and
Erwin were successful; and an act of the provincial assembly
set the place of the first elections and also of the county seat at
"the house of Robert Hanna."

In a remote and primitive wilderness, amid danger from
hostile Indians and wild beasts, the log "house of Robert
Hanna," which had been rented to Joseph Erwin as a tavern
furnishing "Entertainment for Man and Beast," now furnished
formal justice to western Pennsylvania pioneers. In this log
courthouse one small room sufficed for the parties to the disputes, the witnesses, the jury, and the spectators, all of whom
stood up at the trial. The only seats, rough hickory chairs
placed on a crude platform of clapboards, were occupied by
the judges. Soon a jail was added, with the usual machinery
of punishment: a whipping post, stocks, and a pillory. And here
the first murder trial in western Pennsylvania was held. Hugh
H. Brackenridge defended the prisoner, an Indian who had
killed a white man. After the burning of Hannastown in 1782
the court still met for some years in this same house, which
survived the fire. The court was then moved to Greensburg,

where the first sitting took place in January, 1787. Westmoreland was the last county of Pennsylvania to be erected under the proprietors, and the court at the house of Robert Hanna was the only Pennsylvania court in the western section to administer justice in the name of the King of England.

The first court in Pittsburgh was held under the authority of Virginia, which claimed this region as the District of West Augusta. Before the Revolution Lord Dunmore, royal governor of Virginia, had given the name of Fort Dunmore to Fort Pitt. Here in February, 1775, sat the first court for the West Augusta district. And here at the Point a ducking stool was erected for the immersion of offenders in the waters of the two rivers. In 1773, when Pennsylvania set up the new county of Westmoreland, including all of southwestern Pennsylvania below the Ohio and as far east as the mountains, Dunmore appointed Dr. John Connolly of Pittsburgh to challenge the authority of Pennsylvania. Connolly attempted to break up the new county by appearing at Hannastown and dispersing the court. Arthur St. Clair placed Connolly under arrest, but he was soon released. In November, 1775, Connolly was imprisoned for his loyalist activities and took no more part in the boundary dispute. Virginia remained in control of the region now included in Allegheny, Fayette, Greene, and Washington counties until the settlement of the boundary dispute in 1780. Meanwhile Virginia had broken up the region which it claimed into three counties—Yohogania, Ohio, and Monongalia.

When Allegheny County was formed in 1788, the first county court met in Watson's two-story log house at Pittsburgh. A jail was erected with stocks, pillory, and whipping post. After a brief period of meetings in Watson's house this court met in William Irwin's tavern and later at the "Sign of the Waggon," kept by John Reed. It then removed to its home in the new courthouse, where were also held the chief entertainments of the time—amateur theatricals, Punch and Judy shows, tightrope and slack-wire performances.

Trial by jury was known early in these courts—it was established at Hannastown in April, 1773. A jury tried five cases before the Yohogania court in September, 1777. Ordinary cases, however, were tried by justices themselves. Early court sessions were picturesque. Henry Marie Brackenridge has described in his memoirs the first court held in Butler:

"The first court held in Butler drew the whole population to the town, some on account of business, some to *make* business, but the greater part from idle curiosity. They were at that time chiefly Irish, who had all the characteristics of the nation. A log-cabin just raised and covered, but without window-sash, or doors, or daubing, was prepared for the hall of justice. A carpenter's bench with three chairs upon it was the judgment seat. The bar of Pittsburgh attended, and the presiding judge, a stiff, formal, and pedantic old bachelor, took his seat supported by the two associate judges, who were common farmers, one of whom was blind of an eye.

"The hall was barely sufficient to contain the *bench,* bar, jurors, and constables. But few of the spectators could be accommodated on the lower floor, the only one yet laid; many therefore clambered up the walls, and placing their hands and feet in the open interstices between the logs hung there, suspended like enormous Madagascar bats. Some had taken possession of the joists, and big John M'Junkin (who until now had ruled at all public gatherings) had placed a foot on one joist and a foot on another, directly over the heads of their honors, standing with outstretched legs like the Colossus of Rhodes. The judge's sense of propriety was shocked at this exhibition. The sheriff, John M'Candless, was called, and ordered to clear the walls and joists. He went to work with his assistants, and soon pulled down by the legs those who were in no very great haste to obey. M'Junkin was the last."

The earliest judges were not always lawyers, but merely men chosen from the community and referred to as "judges not learned in the law." Although usually known for good judgment and a sense of fairness, they were often as crude as the communities they served or as the houses in which the courts met. These lay judges, or associate judges, were frequently uneducated frontiersmen and petty frontier politicians, who turned out in fringed hunting shirts, leggings, and coonskin caps, and they did not always hold court with suitable dignity.

CANDLE
STICK

They were known to leave the bench and pummel each other roundly, to throw each other bodily out of the court room, to come to court under the influence of liquor, and often not to put in an appearance at all. Lay judges, however, had authority only in the courts held every three months and known as courts of quarter sessions. Visiting justices held the superior courts. They must have made a brave show as, in their flowing robes, they were greeted by the leading gentry and lawyers of the town and marshaled by the sheriff on horseback.

Frontier justice was thus not solely in the hands of crude,

uneducated men. There were more than a few eminent and capable judges and lawyers who studied law under the best legal talent to be found. Judges Alexander Addison and Hugh Henry Brackenridge were cultured and forceful men, as well equipped for the law as their eastern brothers. Such a man, also, was James Ross, a recognized leader of the Allegheny County bar during his time. Addison was a graduate of the University of Aberdeen and a former minister of the Redstone Presbytery. Brackenridge was a Princeton graduate, and Ross obtained his education first under the Reverend John McMillan at Canonsburg and later at Philadelphia.

Frontier courts concerned themselves with such matters as the granting of permits to run ferries and to build water mills, the licensing of taverns and the regulation of their prices, the fining of tavern-keepers for violation of such regulations, the registration of earmarks of cattle and stock, the regulation of road-building, the collection of debts, and disorderliness such as drunken carousing and theft or disputes between individuals. Theft of a pig, of a plow, of plow irons, of two pounds of coffee, of a watch, of six watches from a shop, and of fruit trees are listed in early records. Horse-thieving was one of the most common crimes and, since horses were valuable to the frontiersman, one of the most harshly punished.

Punishment in most cases was severe. Locking in the pillory and ducking were the most common punishments, and every person passing the pillory was allowed to throw one stone at the prisoner. Branding with hot irons and the cutting off of the offender's ears were frequently ordered. But in September, 1776, the Pennsylvania constitution directed that penal laws

PILLORY

be less cruel and that punishment should more nearly fit the crime. In 1790 the penal law was revised and torture done away with. Slaves and servants, however, still received particularly severe sentences. Whipping by as much as a thousand stripes, the application of thumbscrews, and sweating and branding were not uncommon for such classes of offenders. That there was no great care shown in dealing out justice is indicated by the statement of one judge to a prisoner accused of stealing a mare and colt: "We don't know where you got them, nor when, nor how, nor whose they were; but we think you stole them."

Although strong discontent was often voiced in regard to early judges and although punishments were severe and sometimes savage, yet the frontier on the whole settled its disputes with admirable fairness. Times were violent. Questions of all kinds were hotly disputed, for they were important questions in the growth of a new country, and much depended on their settlement. People plunged into legal and political disputes with the same violent energy that they put into the defense of their homes, into their religion, into their dances and their tall tales, and into their friendships and hatreds. When much of the future welfare of a community depended on every decision, each step in the advance had to be given earnest consideration.

The first attempts at organizing political parties in the frontier were taken when signs of the Revolution were definitely threatening, by the committees of correspondence in the region. It was by these committees that the frontier kept in touch with events in the East. Through these committees the frontier patriots acquainted themselves with the acts of their brother pa-

triots in the East and with developments in the threatening re-
volt against the government of Great Britain, which was represented by a great number of Tories about Fort Pitt, and they
studied ways and means of preparing themselves for the struggle that was ahead. The Revolutionary War first raised political questions of major significance on the frontier. The question of allegiance itself was serious. And if the frontier were
to break away from the control of the mother country there
were problems of setting up new governments that must be
considered. The mountains between the frontier and the re-
volting colonies on the seacoast made of the frontier almost a
separate state.

There had been some schooling in politics for the frontier
settlers in the quarrels as to the rightful control of southwestern Pennsylvania between the Virginia groups of West Augusta
and the Pennsylvania groups who had crossed the mountains
from Lancaster and Cumberland to Westmoreland County.
For some time irate farmers met in caucuses in various cabins
throughout the district, arguing, scheming, and debating. Although the two factions joined in the Revolution as ardent
Whigs to root out the Tories, fiery sentiments persisted between them for years.

In 1775 two stormy meetings were held, one at Hannastown
and the other at Pittsburgh, for the purpose of protesting the
actions of Great Britain and encouraging the protection of
American liberty. In the resolutions drawn up at these meetings the frontier was showing its spirit and was sounding
the first angry notes of independence in western Pennsylvania. Then in 1776 Pennsylvania drew up its first constitu-

tion for complete self-government, and the western Pennsylvania representatives to the convention became intense democrats. The rural settlers and the townspeople were concerned over such questions as the Indian ravages to which the frontier was subjected, cheap land and the development of roads west of the mountains, free navigation of the Mississippi —important in connection with the shipping of crops and stock to New Orleans—and the establishment of schools. For years the farmers of western Pennsylvania clung to the Pennsylvania constitution of 1776, which has been called the most democratic in United States history. They seated four delegates in the Council of Censors, a unique body that met every seven years to determine whether or not the constitution had been violated. Between 1776 and 1790 each county sent one representative to the supreme executive council of the state. It was a period of vigorous democracy. The western population was being swollen by a great influx of newcomers from the East, men with eastern capital interested in developing industry now that the frontier was safe for such ventures. Business and trade with eastern merchants and financiers developed, and these men began to work for control of politics in the growing industrial communities west of the mountains. New developments took place in the political organization of the state. Republican and Tammany societies were formed in a number of towns for discussion and for the strengthening of political action.

Political organization, however, remained weak and exceedingly loose until the end of the century. At churches, before and after service, people could be approached and their political beliefs sounded out and directed. A prominent Westmoreland County democrat, William Findley, mingled with the crowds usually to be found at ferries, mills, and distilleries and spread his political ideas among them. Except for muster days, when the militia met under the direction of its Federalist officers, there was no regular method for the control and development of political feeling. The Federalist officers took advantage of muster days to develop their men politically. At a meeting of the Democratic-Republicans in the Meadville courthouse resolutions were drawn up for the devising of "laudable means" for electing Democratic-Republican officers throughout the thirteen regiments of the state militia to counteract the influence of these Federalist officers. It was resolved that each militia company should send representatives to a future meeting to consider the election of officers, especially of the brigadier general and brigade inspector. The democrats were making a good start by centering their attention on the militia.

During the closing years of the century Democratic-Republican sentiment was heightened throughout western Pennsylvania by opposition to the newly established National Bank, and this opposition was linked with the demand for cheap paper money, which the farmers thought would enable them to carry on the growing trade of the district. The Federalists and their leader, Alexander Hamilton, were decidedly unpopular on the developing frontier, which showed strong opposition to the national constitution. The farmers claimed that the constitution was the work of eastern bankers and merchants out of sympathy with the needs of the western agricultural communities. Then Hamilton levied his excise on distilleries and their products, and frontier feeling flared into the Whiskey Insurrection. The Stamp Act, or duty on notes, deeds, and other documents, added fire to the explosion. Violent political meetings sprang up in every town. Stump speeches from angry contestants were shouted simultaneously to the same crowds. Oaths, yells from the listeners, blows, sticks and stones hurtled over the heads of the audiences.

A traveler from the East in 1784 has said that even on the frontier two men could not drink a half gill of whiskey together without discussing a point of politics, to the great improvement and edification of the bystanders. And Johann Schoepf wrote that although these people on the frontier hated the name of a justice, yet they were not transgressors. It was not only the name of a justice that they hated. Like the true Scots that many of them were, they hated even more the name of the excisemen, the men who collected the taxes on distilled liquors, and they protested the appointment and activities of such officers as soon as they were appointed. For some time liberty poles were a favorite form of protest. Around a tall pole or young sapling stripped of its branches crowds assembled to hear fiery speeches, draw up resolutions, and sing the *Ça ira* or the *Carmagnole,* which had come from France with other products of the French Revolution. When the commission appointed to hear the complaints of the whiskey insurgents met at the General Butler Tavern, a number of the insurgents gathered outside and put up a pole, to which was fastened a banner bearing the words "Liberty and no excise, Death to cowards and traitors." The Reverend Robert Ayres in his diary for Friday, August 1, 1794, records the temper of such gatherings at a liberty-tree celebration in Brownsville:

TRIPODS

"I was riding through the town & ere I was aware I came party to about 20 or 30 men erecting a Liberty-tree, I stop'd a minute or 2 and looked: and thence ride towards my own house, but meeting Wm. Evans in the next street, (Market Street) he asked if there were many people at the said tree. I told him perhaps 20 or 30, but, said I, I did not see any of the principal leading people of the Town there; Evans goes right to the s'd tree & informs what I said, which was Immediately exagerated to be entirely worse than what I said; they were much enraged & wrote an imperious letter to me to come down immediately & explain what I had said about the Party assembled at liberty-tree. I first wrote them a note & then at length concluded to go down & speake with them face to face; they appointed a Committee & made much about nothing, & on hearing the Report of the committee the Rabble was satisfied."

Newspapers lost all restraint in their violent partisanship. One editor publicly cowhided another. The *Tree of Liberty*, the Democratic-Republican paper in Pittsburgh, published the following notice:

"Albert Gallatin, the friend of the people, the enemy of tyrants, is to be supported on Tuesday the 14th of October next, for the Congress of the U. S. Fellow citizens, ye who are opposed to speculators, land jobbers, public plunderers, high taxes, 8% loans, and standing armies, vote for Mr. Gallatin." The *Pittsburgh Gazette* sneered at Brackenridge, backer of the *Tree of Liberty*, as "Citizen Brackenridge," deriding what they called the insidious French revolutionary influence in the community. The *Gazette* referred to Brackenridge as the

"Jacobin printer of the *Tree of Liberty, Blasphemy, and Slander*." It also jeered at a dinner given by the leading Democratic-Republicans of the town on the fourth of March, 1802, the anniversary of Jefferson's inauguration. The dinner was given in the tavern of "Citizen" Jeremiah Sturgeon, at the "Sign of the Cross Keys." Toasts were drunk to "Citizen" Thomas Jefferson, "Citizen" Aaron Burr, "Citizen" James Madison, "Citizen" Albert Gallatin, and "Citizen" Thomas McKean.

Modern methods of political control had already been started by a group of Pittsburgh politicians christened the "Clapboardian Democracy" by a member of the Democratic-Republican party who had left the party ranks. Its members constituted the first political ring to attempt to gain control of city and state politics. They were all close neighbors in the city block occupied by the General Butler Tavern, and were given their name from the row of houses in which they lived, known as Clapboard Row from the materials of which the houses were built. All the men were voters, some were office holders, and those who were not, wanted to be. The postmaster, George Adams; his successor, Dr. Hugh Scott; William Gazzam, brigade inspector of the Allegheny County militia and justice of the peace; Thomas Baird, a candidate for burgess in 1803; Joseph McClurg, candidate for supervisor; Samuel Ewalt, on whose lot stood the first log building of the Pittsburgh Academy; Adamson Tannehill, president of the Pittsburgh Fire Company; and Tarleton Bates, co-editor of the *Tree of Liberty*, were all members of the "Clapboardian Democracy." Its opponents were men whose names have been prominent in city history—Colonel James O'Hara, General John Neville,

Major Isaac Craig, Colonel Presley Neville, Major Ebenezer Denny, Dr. George Stevenson, and most of the former Revolutionary officers of the town.

After 1798 a strong political organization was set up in western Pennsylvania to support the democratic movement. Township committees of correspondence were created; and they were headed by county committees of the same kind. These in turn looked for guidance either to a state senatorial district or to the United States congressional district that consisted of all the counties between Pittsburgh and Erie. In 1805 the western Pennsylvania Democratic-Republican party split into a conservative group and a radical group. The most dramatic incident of the political rivalry between these two wings was a duel, in which Tarleton Bates was mortally shot. This frontier democracy, however, was a real force in national political affairs.

Such sharply drawn lines, such violent cleavages between political parties, such unyielding principles may seem rather unreasonable to later generations. They were natural expressions, however, of the spirit of the frontier. The frontiersman had taken his early economic struggles seriously, and he also took his politics seriously.

From Indian Trail to Turnpike

XIV

IN THE summer of 1784 a family of five—father, mother, and three children—with a servant boy of fourteen, left Philadelphia and took the road to the West in typical pioneer fashion.

"We were provided with three horses, on one of which my mother rode carrying her infant, with all the table furniture and cooking utensils. On another were packed the stores of provisions, the plough irons, and other agricultural tools. The third horse was rigged out with a pack saddle, and two large creels, made of hickory withes in the fashion of a crate, one over each side, in which were stored the beds and bedding, and the wearing apparel of the family. In the centre of these creels there was an aperture prepared for myself and sister, and the top was well secured by lacing, to keep us in our places, so that only our heads appeared above. Each family was supplied with one or more cows. . . . Their milk furnished the morning and evening meal for the children, and the surplus was carried in canteens for use during the day."

COW BELL

This was the usual manner of travel for people moving westward. But there were hundreds of other pioneers who,

175

poverty-stricken, had to make the journey on foot. Sometimes the man came first, selected his land, cleared it, planted a first crop in preparation for his family, built the cabin, and then returned East for his wife and children. If he had a wagon he brought his goods in that; if not, he loaded them on a pack horse. If even a pack horse was out of the question, he transported his goods in a pushcart. Sometimes he could hire passage with a professional wagoner, a man who made a business of hauling emigrants over the mountains. Wagoners transported several families at a time, or they carried the belongings of several families, who followed on foot and drove small flocks of sheep, goats, cattle, and poultry. Wagon travel, however, was not common before 1790, as the roads were poor and there was a scarcity of vehicles. In such plodding fashion did freight and persons, mail and news travel between points that were not on navigable streams.

A great system of trails lay ready for the hardy men and women who ventured westward. The trails preferred by the Indians had followed the watersheds, or ridges, wherever possible, because there the forest was more open and free of obstacles, and this fact, together with the height, enabled them to keep a sharp lookout for enemies. It also had the advantage of avoiding swampy ground. Streams were crossed at their mouths, where sand bars usually made the water shallow enough to ford. White travelers at first followed the Indian trails, but as the danger of attack decreased they followed short cuts across low ground; it was easier, also, for wagons to follow the valleys, especially in winter when the ground was frozen, than to labor over the hilltop trails. In their main courses,

WESTWARD

however, the white man's roads followed the Indian trails, and thus some of our great highways were first traversed by the Indians.

Many Indian trails led through western Pennsylvania. At Logstown, on the Ohio River a few miles below Fort Pitt, three trails began. The Mahoning Trail followed the Ohio, the Big Beaver, and the Mahoning rivers into the state of Ohio, where it connected with three important western routes. The Great Trail ran from Logstown to Detroit. The third of these was the Mingo Trail, which crossed the Ohio River at Mingo Bottom, below Steubenville.

From the East five main trails gave entrance to the western country. Into the northwest corner of the state a frontier trail led from the west branch of the Susquehanna River to Tioga Point and the Cowanesque Creek, then across the northwest corner of Potter County to the upper Allegheny. The Shamokin Path ran west along the Susquehanna River and Bald Eagle Creek to the upper waters of the west branch of the Susquehanna at Clearfield; from there it crossed a low divide to the Mahoning Creek, which flows into the Allegheny near Kittanning.

The Frankstown Path, or Kittanning Trail, was known as "the main road to Allegheny." It followed the Juniata River and its Frankstown branch to Kittanning Gap; then across country to Canoe Place and thence to Kittanning. The eastern end of this road is now in part the William Penn Highway.

The Raystown Path followed the Raystown branch of the Juniata and crossed the mountains to Loyalhanna Creek. Along this path was constructed the Pennsylvania Road, con-

necting Lancaster, Bedford, Ligonier, and Fort Pitt. This road
is now the Lincoln Highway. A popular alternate route to the
western end of the Pennsylvania Road was the Glade Road.
It left the Pennsylvania Road about four miles from Bedford
and ran southwest through a district known to early travelers
as the Glades. It passed near modern Somerset and Mt. Pleasant
to Simeral's Ferry, or West Newton, on the Youghiogheny
River, where a boat was taken for Pittsburgh, Ohio, and
Kentucky.

The Nemacolin Trail crossed southwestern Pennsylvania
from Wills Creek on the upper Potomac to the Youghiogheny.
The first military forces used it in crossing the Allegheny
mountains, and it became Braddock's road on his ill-fated
expedition. At the end of a branch of this road, a stone fort
and trading post was established at the mouth of Redstone
Creek, now Brownsville. It was the Braddock Road, connecting
Cumberland, Maryland, with the Ohio River, at Wheeling,
that gave to Cumberland the name "Key of the Mountains."
And it is this road that is now traveled by motorists as the
National Highway.

Some idea of the nature of these trails can be had when we
realize that neither Braddock nor Forbes could cross the Alleghenies until men with axes had widened the Indian and pack
horse trails to allow the passage of wagons. By the time the
great movement of pioneering set in, these roads had become
so clogged with fallen timber and new growth that in many
places they had to be reopened for pack horse traffic. Only a
few feet wide, the early roads wound from the East over hills
and level stretches until the rugged ranges of the Alleghenies

PACKHORSE TRAIN

were reached. Here the trails led through oak-covered gorges, climbed craggy ridges, along ledges of dizzy height, or crawled under hanging rocks.

Along such trails wound the pack trains in single file; the foremost horse was ridden by the man in charge, and each following animal was tied to the packsaddle of the horse in front. A driver followed on the last horse to watch and adjust the packs and to sting with the crack of his whip those beasts disposed to lag. A pack train of from ten to fifteen horses, each carrying two hundred pounds burden, could in this way be managed by two men. So great was the traffic along these roads before wagons became common that at convenient places of rest as many as five hundred pack horses were counted at one time. Travelers encountered at every few miles East-bound trains of pack horses heavily burdened with whiskey, peltry, and ginseng, the three main articles sent to the East. Those going toward Pittsburgh were loaded with salt and bales of dry goods, or with hardware.

By the end of the pack train era enough settlers had taken up lands to demand "improved" roads for wheeled vehicles. On all these roads could be used the first crude, springless, stage wagons—light coaches slung on leather straps, enclosed at the sides and ends by curtains of canvas or leather that could be raised or lowered to let in the air or protect the travelers from rain. These usually held three roomy seats inside and one outside for the coachman and two passengers, thus carrying twelve persons in all. When mail pouches were carried inside the stage, the passengers were limited to eight.

Such travel could be quite tolerable, although frequently an axletree broke and passengers had to wait for an oncoming coach. Sometimes they were forced to walk several miles with their luggage before a stagecoach could be found, and then they had to crowd in as best they could. A stage occasionally overturned; this was bad enough by day when the weather was fair, but when it happened at night in rain or snow the passengers were forced to kindle a fire in the woods and huddle about it. To prevent such accidents and to give balance to a swaying stage, drivers would call to the passengers to lean out of the stage first at one side, then at the other, to avoid upsetting in deep ruts. "Now, gentlemen, to the right," a driver would call, upon which all passengers stretched themselves out of the carriage to balance that side. "Now, gentlemen, to the left." This was said to have happened on one occasion at least a dozen times in half that number of miles. At points where the mire was deep, drivers with trousers rolled up joined team to team to help each other in pulling their loads forward. At times they took down fences and made new roads through the fields.

The glory and pride of the early roads were the Conestoga wagons, or, as they were called at times, the Pitt teams or turnpike schooners. Schooners they were, sweeping in great flotillas over mountain roads, colorful as any Spanish galleon. Between fields of ripening wheat and wind-shaken forests, drawn by their six-horse teams, they lumbered (said the chroniclers of that day) without creak or groan, so perfectly were they adjusted to road and freight.

The horses that drew these wagons, well-matched blacks, bays, or dappled grays, were handsome, active animals with great powers of endurance, legs short rather than long, short arched necks, and full manes. Although their stride was short it carried them steadily forward and was sturdy and safe in descending long mountain roads. They could pull their load of six tons or more from twelve to fourteen miles a day. They were originally bred, according to tradition, from Flemish stallions and Virginia mares.

Horse, wagon, and driver were worthy of one another. Together they made up one of the finest means of transport in the history of trade. The driver, if he was one of the better types in his class, took a just and poetic pride in his equipment. He knew that his wagon was built with the finest adjustment of materials and parts—white oak for the frame, hickory for axletrees and singletrees, gum tree for the hubs, and poplar for the boards. The body of the wagon was long, about twenty-four feet, and deep, with a sag in the middle from end to end and from side to side, so that if the load shifted with the lean of the wagon it settled in the center instead of pressing against the sides or back. The bows over which the white homespun covering was drawn, curving up and outward from the side-boards, rose eleven feet from the ground and overhung the ends like great bonnets to keep out dust and rain. As all parts were turned and pared to a nice balance between strength and lightness, they were everywhere reënforced with iron, not merely practical reënforcements, but wrought painstakingly into designs of hearts, tulips, snakes, or knob ends. At the rear of the wagon hung the tool box, the particular pride of the driver, with ornamental hasps and hinges beautifully chiseled from iron. From the rear axletree hung the water bucket.

These picturesque freighters were driven, when the driver

CONESTOGA WAGON

was not walking or sitting astride his saddle horse (the wheel horse on the left side), from the lazy board, which projected between the wheels on the left of the wagon. Conestoga drivers thus originated the American practice of passing to the right in traffic. So proud were they of their horses' appearance that they equipped them with bearskin or gaudily fringed woolen housings and adorned the bridles with loops of red trimmings. And over the hames of each harness rose an arch of open, well-toned bells of iron, bronze, or brass, four or five to an arch. Bells were at first a necessity on narrow wooded roads to warn of approach; but with the widening and improvement of road beds they were kept for decoration and for their pleasant, jingling tunes. When a wagoner in distress on the road was helped by another, the helper received the hame bells as a reward.

The materials and design of these wagons made them unbreakable on roads that were deeply rutted and filled with rocks and jutting boulders; roads that were obstructed by stumps and spreading roots; roads that sloped to one side and were washed out by storms and overflowing streams, and that led in places through swamps.

When the road from the Cumberland Valley to Pittsburgh was cleared and widened between 1785 and 1790, these turnpike schooners began to appear, bearing freight of iron, salt, and other necessities, as well as families of settlers, to the West, and "back-loading" to the East with furs and skins, flour and wheat. Until their great age passed, about 1830, they came and went in increasing numbers until as many as three thousand at a time—a gorgeous parade in vermilion, soft blue, and white, bells jangling, whips cracking, men singing and cursing—were rolling uphill and down, their white covers bleached whiter in the sun.

Finding lodgings for a night was not always easy for travelers. The Reverend David McClure described this difficulty when he came over the Alleghenies. McClure and his companion, on horseback, had traveled late into the night through mud and mire and through streams up to their horses' bellies, with the rain pouring down. One settler, Andrew Byerly, refused to let them in when they knocked at his door and asked for a night's shelter. After riding on to the next cabin they were at first met with a like answer. The owner told them through his closed door that his cabin was already filled with traders and drovers. But at their pleading he relented, opened his door to them, and allowed them to spend the night.

"Around the dirty room of the log house lay asleep and snoaring, a number of men. No bed or bedding was to be had. We persuaded the fellow who let us in, to make up a fire, we were obliged however, to bring in the wood, & we partly dried our clothes. He also brought us two dirty blankets, & spreading them on the muddy floor, before the fire, we lay down supperless to try to sleep. But such swarms of fleas from the blankets attacked us on all quarters, that sleep refused us its oblivious soothing comforts."

As the number and frequency of uninvited guests in wayside cabins grew, the involuntary host found himself becoming innkeeper, especially if he owned a fair-sized cabin or log or stone house. Then, as innkeeper, he acquired in turn a number of other offices. He was the one person who was always paid in cash for service and in consequence became a kind of frontier banker. Letters were left with him for other travelers expected to pass that way; so he became also a kind of postmaster. Travelers brought him the most recent newspapers and wayfarers handed out gossip picked up along the road, and by these means he became a kind of news agent.

The terms "inn" and "tavern" are not always interchangeable in speaking of early hostelries. In New York and New England, "tavern" was more often used; in Pennsylvania, "inn" was more common. In the South the term "ordinary" was habitual. "Tavern" and "inn" were sometimes used to distinguish, respectively, between mere drinking places and establishments where meals and lodging were provided. Some localities scorned the term "inn" as too English.

In his journal, an early traveler warned his readers not to be deceived by the bare name of "tavern." The people, he said, kept tavern if they had anything over and above what they used; if not, the traveler looked out for himself.

Another traveler arrived at the cabin of a smith "who on occasion plays the innkeeper." But his house was no inn that evening. He had nothing to eat, and the traveler was compelled to "grope for two miles more." At a later stage he stopped at another cabin. On inquiry, he was told that the owner kept no tavern, but he was taken in willingly and found better accommodations than if it had been one.

When Schoepf was driving over the Forbes Road in his chaise, he stopped one evening at the cabin of a Dr. Peter, a German. The doctor was absent, looking for his pigs gone astray in the woods. But his wife, "a good little old woman, and energetic," gave the horses oats and set before the travelers mountain tea and maple sugar, "which as well as her bacon, whiskey and cakes were the products of her own land and industry."

When Dr. Robert Wellford traveled through western Pennsylvania in 1794 he breakfasted one morning at Mrs. Woodrow's, the most comfortable house he had seen in the region. One large room was divided by plank partitions into three sleeping rooms and one eating room, with a very large log fire; the kitchen was under the same roof. The doctor's comment was: "If this was the best house, judge then of the others."

It was customary for roadside dwellers to offer a floor for sleeping and to allow lodgers to prepare their own food. One lodger records that his party arrived at a large tavern where, if one brought meat and drink along with him, he found room enough to dispose of them. Two young fellows here kept house, but had nothing except whiskey and cheese; bread and meat were "accidental articles."

The typical Pennsylvania inn, after the earliest days, was usually built of stone, often almost square, with perhaps an extension in the rear. It was seldom more than two stories in height, usually with a two-storied porch at the rear or side and an attic with windows in the gable ends. Two doors opened off the long porch stretched across the front of the building—one to the taproom, which became the neighborhood resort for settlers from miles around, and the other into a hall that led to the inn parlor and family living quarters.

Three distinct classes of inns developed to serve three distinct classes of people. Drovers stopped at inns away from villages or towns. There they obtained food and shelter for

TAVERN

themselves, and pasture, water, and feed for their animals. At one mountain inn, during one night, there were counted more than thirty six-horse teams in the wagon yard, one hundred Kentucky mules in the barnyard, and one thousand hogs in another enclosure, and as many fat cattle and sheep were pastured in the fields round about. Such a cavalcade had put up at only one inn on one road for the night. What a procession must have moved the next day when all the inns and taverns along the roads had discharged their customers.

PIGGIN

A slightly better type of inn catered to wagoners and the poorer class of settlers. The wagoner, after putting his wagon in the yard and his horses in the stable, washed up at the pump. Then, leaving his blankets in the taproom, he went in to supper. The meal might consist of ham and eggs, beefsteak, fried speckled trout, fried potatoes and griddlecakes, preserves, pickles, pie, cheese, cake, and coffee. For such a meal he paid twelve and half cents or half a shilling. After an evening of rude merriment at the bar, the wagoner spread his blankets on the taproom floor and spent the night there. The landlord gave him this right as well as that of using as much wood as he cared to burn, in consideration of the money he had spent.

Inns catering to stagecoach passengers were of the best grade. Appetizing, indeed, were the meals served. The landlord sat at one end of the table to carve the roasts. At the opposite end his wife or a guest served other dishes. The guests helped themselves to what was not served from the head and foot of the table. There was no limit on "refills." The table was loaded with boiled mutton, boiled ham, hot roast turkey, mashed potatoes, boiled onions, creamed turnips, coleslaw, celery, two

or three kinds of pickles, four or five kinds of jellies and preserves, hot rolls, biscuits, and wheat bread. The guest had to
eat everything on his plate to make room for the mince pie,
custard pie, apple pie, pound cake, suet pudding, doughnuts,
tea, and coffee that would follow for dessert. Such a meal cost
twenty-five cents.

Inn bedrooms frequently contained six and eight beds, and
when the inn was crowded each bed did service for three persons. An English traveler, Hulme, wrote of early inns:

"Very good accomodations for travellers the whole of the
way. The stage stops to breakfast and to dine, and sleeps where
it sups. They literally feasted us everywhere, at every meal,
with venison and good meat of all sorts: everything in profu-
sion. In one point, however, I must make an exception, with
regard to some houses: at night I was surprised, in taverns so
well kept in other respects, to find bugs in the beds! I am
sorry to say I observed (or, rather, *felt*,) this too often. Always
good eating and drinking, but not always good sleeping."

As inn accommodations improved, the innkeeper and host
developed into a definite type and personage. Henry M. Brackenridge described these men:

"The landlords or tavern-keepers are, in reality, the only
lords we have in Pennsylvania; they possess a degree of intelligence and respectability of character which justly gives them
an influence *dans la chose publique,* which very little cor-
responds with that of mine host in the country of John Bull,
which may account for the good jokes of British travelers on
our keepers of public houses, in respect to their political and
military importance. Before my time, BLACK CHARLES kept the

first hotel in the place; when I can first remember, the sign of GENERAL BUTLER, kept by Patrick Murphy, was the *head tavern;* and afterward the GREEN TREE, on the bank of the Mononga- hela, kept by William Morrow. The General Butler was con- tinued by Molly Murphy for some years after the death of Paddy; she was the friend of my boyhood and youth, and, al- though as rough a Christian as I ever knew, I verily believe that a better Christian heart, one more generous and benevo- lent, as well as sturdy and fearless, never beat in Christian bos- om. Many an orphan, many a friendless one, many a wretched being has shed, in secret, the tear of gratitude over the memory of Molly Murphy!"

Inns and taverns were identified and frequently became famous by their quaint names. These names were announced by signboards hung over the doorway or from a post near the door. Tavern signs were frequently beautiful designs in wrought iron or on painted boards. At Brownsville the "Sign of the Globe" was a famous eating house. At Brownsville, too, was the "Sign of the Cross Keys," a curious displacement of a religious symbol used by the church, the keys of St. Peter. The "Sign of the Buck," "Indian Queen," "Black Horse," "Fountain Inn," "Mermaid," "Rising Sun," "Sign of the White Goose," and "Spread Eagle" appeared as names of taverns in various quarters. Names of popular heroes were also given to inns; the "Sign of Gen. George Washington" was a favorite stopping place, as was the "Sign of Gen. Wayne."

It had been along the main watercourses that the first traders and missionaries penetrated the region. As settlers came in increasing numbers these waterways continued to be used.

Up the Youghiogheny and the Monongahela they came; down the Allegheny from Connecticut and New York, via Erie; and over the Juniata from the Susquehanna. Pittsburgh was a meeting point for all these routes; and so, since it was also at the head of the Ohio River, it was the gateway to the farther West. Brownsville, too, was a transfer point from overland to water travel, as was West Newton for the same traffic from the Potomac. Conemaugh, now part of Johnstown, and Kittanning served similar offices between the Juniata and the Conemaugh-Kiskiminetas rivers, which carried traffic to the Allegheny and thence to Pittsburgh. As more remote sections were opened for settlement, the earlier portages became the keys to lines of trade and travel. These portages the traders and hunters had established as the shortest or most convenient land routes from one waterway to another. From the Hudson-Mohawk system in New York, New Englanders entered northwestern Pennsylvania. From the Susquehanna and Juniata system settlers came across the broad mountain barrier, and from the Potomac-Monongahela system to the south they entered from Maryland and Virginia.

Travelers could follow no water route without doing some travel by land. For example, from New York a traveler west bound for Pittsburgh might take a boat up the Hudson to Albany, a voyage of three or four days; then proceed by wagon to Schenectady, by bateau up the Mohawk River to Rome, New York, from there overland to Wood Creek, then by boat through Oneida Lake, down the Oswego River to Lake Ontario, by boat to Niagara, by wagon to Buffalo on Lake Erie, by boat to Presque Isle, or the town of Erie. From there he could

FLATBOAT

take a road that led through Waterford and Meadville to Pittsburgh, or he might embark upon a keel boat at Waterford and descend French Creek and the Allegheny River to Pittsburgh.

The earliest water craft were dugouts and bark canoes. Used originally by the Indians, they were later adopted by white settlers as their first means of river transport. The dugout canoe, or pirogue, was a sycamore or cypress log hollowed by burning or with the adz. Sometimes the dugouts were split lengthwise and planks were inserted to widen them. They could be built large enough to accommodate thirty or forty men and as much as forty tons of freight. They were steered by a stern oar and propelled by poles, or sometimes by sails or oars.

The bateaux mentioned by so many early travelers on the western waters included craft of many kinds. Usually, however, the bateaux were flat, keelless boats made of planks, tapering at the ends. They were sometimes equipped with cabins and might be propelled by oars, poles, or sails. Sails were employed on many types of craft on the three rivers. The most common means of downstream transportation was the flatboat, sometimes called the ark or broadhorn, built somewhat like a modern houseboat, although cruder. It was usually about fifteen feet wide and fifty feet long. It depended upon the current for its impetus but could be managed in a clumsy fashion by great oars that extended out at each side and at the back.

What the Conestoga wagon was to the mountain road, the keel boat was to the Ohio River. It was king of the river, although a gypsy king, to be sure. It was a slender, pointed boat, which because of its light draft could navigate shallow streams. But its great service lay in its navigability upstream

over currents and riffles. Travelers used keel boats for making
quick journeys, and merchants found them the safest and most
dependable of all the boats on the rivers. Because of their speed,
there was less chance of perishable goods spoiling, and they
were manned by experienced fellows who knew every trick of
navigation. From the keel, covered with plank, rose the ribs,
also plank-covered, with low gunwales. A cargo box was erected
over the deck with a footpath all the way around. These keel
boats were about ten by sixty feet, and carried twenty to forty
tons of freight.

As keel boats were returned up river—unlike flatboats, which
were broken up for firewood at the end of their journey—
various methods of propelling them were used. When the
current was not too deep, setting poles, twelve to twenty feet
long and shod with iron, were struck in the river bed; then
the boatmen pressed their weight against the poles, sometimes
leaning so far forward that they crept on their hands and toes
the length of the gangway, four men on each side. Sometimes
the men on the shore side used poles while the men on the
river side rowed. When the current was too deep for setting
poles, the cordelle, or towing rope, was used to draw the boat
upstream. This rope might be several hundred feet long. One
end was made fast to the boat, and the other end was taken
ashore by men who tramped through brush, waded, and swam
inlets as they pulled the boat up river. Sometimes parties went
ahead with axes to clear the way and with rifles on their backs
as protection from Indians. Warping was another method of
cordelling. A skiff carried one end of the cordelle upstream,
where it was fastened to a snag or a tree. The other end was

KEELBOAT

drawn by the crew around a capstan or windlass, or sometimes
hand over hand. In this way six miles were made in a day. At
high water, when the boat was navigating near trees whose
branches overhung the current, bushwacking was resorted to.
Each man in turn, from the bow, seized a branch and walked
aft. At the stern he released the branch and returned around
the cargo box to the bow, from where he began the operation
again.

The braggarts who manned the keel boats have taken their
place in legend as iron-muscled giants in scarlet shirts and blue
jackets, leather caps or wide, flop-brimmed hats. They were
usually bearded and moccasined, armed with knives and
equipped with tobacco pouches. They were bruisers and rascals
who performed great exploits on river and shore, according to
their own reports and according to reports from others. They
were heavy drinkers and frolickers, singers and fighters, card-
playing, roistering, jigging ex-soldiers of the Revolution in
search of further adventure. Or they might be former Indian
scouts grown restless since the frontier had become safe from
raids. Sometimes they were from farms that had proven unyielding or too tame.

The keel boat age was the age of river pageantry, when from
the upper reaches of the Monongahela above Brownsville
down to Natchez and New Orleans the widening expanse of
water was broken by the most picturesque craft that ever
rippled a river; when the air was rent every hour of the day
by brawling shouts and oaths and newly invented epithets, by
songs of boatmen, by shouts of children who played on the
roofs of the lumbering arks and by the screams of mothers

RIVER FRONT

frightened lest they fall into the water. From the flatboats the air was shattered by the whinnying of horses and the mooing of cattle, and rasped by the cackle of geese. From these same flat-boats smoke rose from the fires at which women cooked family meals. Fifty-foot canoes swayed and tilted their cargo at one end, a settler's family at the other. From the great ship-like barges sixty feet long, propelled by twenty or thirty oars, so that they looked like giant water skippers, came the feeble whine of fiddles. And through all this pageant wove the keel boats, passing by the bulkier, blunter, more awkward craft, while the red-shirted, blue-jacketed keelboatmen thumbed their noses and jeered.

Boat building for rivermen and the manufacturing of saddles and harness for drivers gave early Pittsburgh a business-like air. There was a fine trade in lumber, tar, and leather; and numbers of carpenters, millwrights, and workmen made streets and wharves bustle from Brownsville down through McKees-port to the Point.

Pittsburgh early proved its right to the title of Gateway to the West. It became the junction of overland travel from the East and river traffic to the West. The residents of the thriving city became accustomed to great numbers of boats docking at its wharves. At low water as many as a hundred boats, each carrying a family of emigrants, would dock along the Monon-gahela between Pittsburgh and New Geneva, and an equal number along the Allegheny. Larger boats than river craft were built in the vicinity. In 1793 a schooner built between Browns-ville and Pittsburgh sailed to New Orleans and from there to Philadelphia. In the same year packets operating between

Pittsburgh and Cincinnati were made bullet proof and were armed with small cannon. Arrangements were also made whereby passengers and crew could fire through portholes at marauders, white as well as red.

By 1810 shipbuilding had become an important industry. The government built two armed galleys to be used in case of trouble with the Spaniards in Louisiana, who were hampering American trade on the lower Mississippi. The Tarasçon Brothers and other merchants exported goods in seagoing vessels to New Orleans and thence to Philadelphia.

Tarleton Bates had written to a friend on May 25, 1798:

"On Saturday the nineteenth, precisely at 2 P. M., the *first* galley was launched at this place. It was said to be a very beautiful launch, she slid a most unusual distance, I believe 126 feet. When she descends the river is not known, as it depends more on the destinies than on man, for although she is not in a sailing state, neither is the water high enough to admit it."

Two schooners, the "Pittsburgh" and the "Amity," two hundred and seventy tons and one hundred tons respectively, were launched in 1803, and cleared with cargoes of flour for St. Thomas in the Virgin Islands and for Lisbon. Between 1802 and 1805 three schooners, three brigs, and four ships were launched.

In 1804 boats conveying flour from Pittsburgh to New Orleans carried two hundred and fifty to three hundred barrels each. One company sent twenty-five thousand barrels to the South in one year. It is estimated that during that same period one hundred thousand tons of manufactured articles were shipped to the same destination. The quantity of goods carried was increasing at the rate of about two thousand tons annually.

Settlers along the rivers offered a good market for goods of all descriptions. Traders equipped boats with staples and manufactured goods and floated down the rivers peddling their stock. The store boats, as such craft were called, signaled their approach by several loud blasts from a horn. For goods, the settlers bartered cotton, tobacco, flour, grain, pelts, and the like. As many as four and five of these store boats passed in a day. They also carried families into new territory. Emigrants from the East, having arrived in Pittsburgh by Conestoga wagon, sometimes bought and outfitted such boats and, after cruising down the rivers, sold the boats when they had found a desirable spot in which to found a new home.

In the years immediately following the frontier period, show boats plied the western waters. The first of these made its appearance in 1815 when a man named Drake launched the first "opera boat." A decade later an English actor named William Chapman came to Pittsburgh with his family of six, all actors, and launched a show boat that became famous on all the middle western rivers.

Many dangers threatened boats traveling the inland waters. Channels sometimes shifted suddenly, or in spring the melting snows flooded them. Mud banks and sand bars appeared overnight and boats were continually running upon them. Logs caught by one end in the mud of the river bottom tore holes in the bottoms and sides of the boats. The greatest menace, however, were the white outlaws and Indians who frequently plundered solitary boats. Near Shawneetown, on the Ohio River in what is now southern Illinois, lived a notorious gang of outlaws who attacked any boat running aground on the adjacent shoals. After killing the occupants they took the boats downstream to New Orleans and sold them.

Delivery of mail to the frontier was irregular and undependable. All available means of transportation were used. In early days written messages were given into the hands of any one going in the general direction of the place of address—traders, pack-horse men, Indian runners, army couriers, or ordinary travelers. In this way a letter passed through many hands and took a long time to reach its destination. Kenny says in his journal: "Sent my letters off with Ensign Hutchins he going to Bedford on his way to Carolina." Innkeepers served as postmasters, giving to their departing guests letters to be delivered. Letters were laid on the tables of inns, and there they sometimes remained for days until they were examined and paid for.

When the government was firmly organized, regular mail carriers, or post riders, served the frontier. In the *Pittsburgh Gazette* of October 7, 1786, appeared a Philadelphia letter containing the following notice: "Mr. Brison is just returned from New-York with orders to establish a post from this place [*Philadelphia*] to Pittsburgh." This notice meant the breakdown of isolation; it meant that the frontier would be drawn into constant and quicker communication with the more cultured East. But the service was not established until 1788. On July 3 of that year a fortnightly service was established between Pittsburgh and Chambersburg. From the latter place the post traveled weekly to Philadelphia. The duties of the frontier post rider were many and various. His primary job was, of course, to deliver the letters and packages he carried in the portmanteau, slung over his horse's back. One of his duties was to inspect and report the conditions of the roads at ferries and fords. Another was to help any one he might meet on the road who needed his assistance. Still other services he performed were to transfer money from point to point and to return horses for travelers. Post riders were paid in accordance with the weight of mail carried. This led to a certain amount of cheating; sham bundles of straw, or "cheaps," were tied to sealed packets or letters. Wages suffered from private competition with wagon drivers, who could underquote the post riders' price for delivery of mail. It is told of one early Pennsylvania post rider that he supplemented his regular duties by knitting mittens and socks as he jogged along the road.

With the development of roads, mail service improved. In 1794 a post rider began service to Wheeling from Pittsburgh by way of Canonsburg and Washington. In 1798 a mail route began between Pittsburgh and Zanesville, Ohio. As early as 1796 private service began between Pittsburgh and Erie. John Scull, the editor of the *Gazette,* announced with the opening of the road, "A careful person is employed to go from this place to Presqu'Isle, once every two weeks. He will leave the printing office at ten o'clock. Those who wish to write a letter to their friends in that quarter may do so." About 1792 boats began to carry mail on the Ohio. Mail was also carried on river packets, but delivery was much slower than by stage. In 1801 biweekly service was begun through Beaver to northwestern Ohio.

From 1799 to 1814 a one-page letter cost eight cents postage if sent under forty miles. For more than five hundred miles, postage cost thirty-five cents. The usual rate from Philadelphia to Pittsburgh was seventeen cents per sheet. One of the John Thaw letters gives interesting light on postal service at the turn of the century:

"Permit me now to advise when ever you write to any one per post never to make two pieces of paper of a letter when one is sufficient, as with the one to me altho' totally blank on one side you enclosed in another blank, for which I had to pay double postage 3 s which you can refund when you receive this, as its allways customary for a person to pay the postage of Letters when on Bussiness entirely their own."

Letters were not enclosed in envelopes, nor stamped. The single sheet was folded, sealed with wax, and the address was written on the back along with the amount of postage to be collected from the receiver.

Although by this time mail could be rapidly sent between towns such as Chambersburg, Pittsburgh, and Wheeling, often several months were required for it to reach the distant West and Southwest. It was seventy-eight days from the time President Monroe's message to Congress was published, in 1819, until it was read in Little Rock, Arkansas.

When Cramer's *Pittsburgh Magazine Almanack* announced in 1804 the arrival on Monday and Thursday of each week of the "Pittsburgh Good Intent" mail coach from Philadelphia, travel and transport across the Pennsylvania mountains had lost much of its earlier inconvenience and danger, time had been cut down, and passage could be had for twenty dollars. News, goods, and passengers could pass easily now from western Pennsylvania to the eastern seaboard. Life beyond the mountains was therefore more attractive. The roughest pioneering was finished; the first cabins had multiplied into settlements, and settlements had grown into towns. Business men in the East, began to look toward western Pennsylvania as a good place to make fortunes, so they came to places like Pittsburgh, Washington, or Uniontown, established their banks and industries, developed the natural resources, and created a new industrial empire.

BUTTERNUT

Life in the Towns

XV

PITTSBURGH is a fine Country Town . . . possesses toler-able good & cheap markets, dear stores & bad society the In-habitants being so much Engrossed with political discussions that those of oppisite sentiments can hardly think or speak well of each other—its a place by no means so enticeing as Philad^a & a person comeing from thence should do it under the convic-tion of making money & bettering his circumstances, but not of Enjoying the pleasure either of a country or city life."

Thus was Pittsburgh described in a letter written by John Thaw in 1804, and that description would also apply in gen-eral, to those other towns that had grown up in western Penn-sylvania, which only a quarter century before had been largely wilderness. The point of view of the business man from the East expresses the opinion that we ourselves would have held of these communities—towns "by no means so enticeing" as Philadelphia, towns "Engrossed with political discussions," country towns most of them, with the advantages and disad-vantages that such a description implies.

Mr. Thaw in that same year wrote another letter, in which he said that the houses in Pittsburgh numbered four or five hundred, were generally two stories high, and that the old ones were principally of log and the new ones of brick construction. The streets, he said, were straight and narrow but not paved and, of course, were extremely muddy. He spoke of the family pride and of the distinction between classes. He was writing of the frontier metropolis.

These observations show that the frontier was moving beyond the forks of the Ohio River, which, when Captain Trent built his first rude fort there a half century before, had been its extreme edge. A man living when Mr. Thaw wrote might have erected his cabin in actual wilderness, and before he reached old age he would have seen the frontier transformed into a network of roads that led past prosperous farms into any one of a score of thriving towns. He might have ground his corn in a hominy block when he was a young married man; in his later years he could have it ground at a steam mill. He might have made his first journey over the mountains on foot, but before he had grandchildren he could have returned for a visit by regular stage. Settlers had arrived in sufficient numbers to establish such towns as Pittsburgh, Erie, Meadville, Butler, Washington, Uniontown, Brownsville, Connellsville, and Greensburg, besides a hundred villages at points between these towns. What had been wilderness had, through the labors of the pioneers, become civilization when Mr. Thaw arrived in Pittsburgh. In western Pennsylvania men no longer plowed their fields under armed guards as protection from Indians. The stations and forts to which settlers had once fled from attack were falling into decay. No longer was the pack horse the most serviceable means of carrying freight, nor were moccasins and linsey the best wearing apparel. People no longer had to meet in groves or in cabin "praying societies" to worship. Nor did they have to try court cases at Hannastown if they lived in the triangle between the Allegheny and Monongahela rivers. Jerk and johnnycake were staples of diet now only in backward communities.

Gristmills and sawmills, iron works, and distilleries and tanneries had developed like lusty youngsters from the small industries of the settlers, and communities had grown up around them. Conveniences of trade and the heightened standard of living brought organization of town life with markets, courthouses, libraries, and theaters. Connellsville became a thriving town of store keepers and tradesmen, mechanics and innkeepers. Brownsville supported many mills, for corn grinding, for sawing lumber, for fulling and carding wool, and for oil making. Stores developed and taverns were opened. John Gilpin visited Brownsville in 1809 and mentioned the fact that the town boasted eighteen stores. These outfitted a large number of migrants, or "flitters," as they were called, who were on the road to the farther West.

"Generally poor they get here as well as they can, & encamp on the bank of the river & furnish themselves with a boat—the scarcity of this article & the tardiness of the winter often causes them to remain a considerable time & sometimes numerous families have passed the whole winter in their tents or huts to be ready for the earliest breaking of the frost & rising of the waters."

Washington, by 1794, was a considerable town of frame buildings, clapboarded, and "chiefly painted red," except the

WATER MILL

courthouse and two or three other buildings, which were of stone. The appearance of the place was very pleasing to James Elliot, who passed through in that year, because it reminded him of a New England town. He added that the houses in general throughout Pennsylvania were built of brick or stone, but we must remember that he kept pretty well to the main roads.

Harmony (near Zelienople) had been well built soon after 1800 by the Harmonites under the leadership of the Rapps. The red brick buildings housed tanning, dyeing, weaving, carpentering, blacksmithing, and other industries. The town had a botanical garden as well as its vegetable gardens and orchards. And it had what few if any other towns had—a church orchestra of three violins, a violincello, a clarinet, a flute, and two French horns.

Greensburg by 1804 was a pleasant town of one hundred dwelling houses, a German Reformed Church, a courthouse of brick, "and a prison." It also had a post office. To Greensburg many dandies from the surrounding country flocked to see the public races, coming even from Pittsburgh to enjoy the sports and the hospitality of the town's leading citizens and its five inns.

Bedford in the 1790's was a town chiefly of log houses two stories high. To one traveler the inhabitants appeared to be a "heathenish, groveling sort of people, mostly Irish." Although a county seat, there was not a church in it. But to Johann Schoepf, who astonished all settlers along the road by traveling over the mountains in a chaise, it was an agreeable stopping place, regularly planned, with a courthouse and two houses of worship, "which cannot be called churches, being only wooden huts." It was a small town, but as Schoepf said, "a little town in a great wilderness may easily please without beauty."

And so might any of the earliest towns have been described —these clusters of brick or log houses set down far apart "in a great wilderness," with their muddy streets, over which a few thoughtful house owners had perhaps laid occasional planks or a few scattered flagstones and loose bricks. If in summer the streets were pleasant with shade from trees planted along them, they were also grass-grown and weedy and afforded not only pasture for cows and sheep, but also a running ground for pigs and dogs, and were frequently cluttered with drays drawn in from the country by oxen. They were dark streets by night, brightened only occasionally by a lantern swung from a tavern door or a signpost.

Along the mud streets houses ranged themselves according to the fancy of the builders—some of frame with their ends to the street; others of brick, built lengthwise, and with open yards between. Over them stood poplars and willows, interspersed with street wells and pumps. Merchants usually lived with their families in the houses where they carried on business, and over their doorways swung signs announcing their names, signs often as curious as the names of the inns and taverns.

Getting land in the towns was not a question of tomahawk rights or patents, but of buying real estate. Of this business, too, Mr. Thaw wrote to his father to explain why he wanted a loan a year or so after he arrived in Pittsburgh:

"As I deem it proper for you to be acquainted with the reason

STREET SCENE

of this urgency and what I am doing at this distance from my parents I have to Inform you, that this day I have purchased at Sheriffs sale, a new two story Brick House standing on one of the most improveing streets in Pittsburgh 20 ft front by 32 ft deep, the lot 63 ft in depth with a 4 ft alley leading into 3d st passing the adjoining corner house fronting Wood st. This house, cost the person (now dead) who built it, about 2500 $ and the Lots adjoining of same size and value are let at Two Dlls per foot. . . . Wood street is the handsomest in the place, it is now paved from the river up to 3rd st and the next square on which my house stands will be done next year."

As to rents and removals, Mr. Thaw had written earlier:

"Removals generally takes place here the first of April & the population being equal to the dwelling houses, makes it very difficult to get one at this time, and also causes rents to be as high as with you. After looking in vain for a suitable house —I have taken one near the Bank but in an unfinished state at Eight Dlls per month in this I am now living & collecting the necessary apparatus for housekeeping—the house not being comfortable I intend moveing as soon as I can procure another, have one now in view, that will be finished in a few weeks, it is a very convenient two story Building, rents at 150 $ & dont expect to get one for much less."

Mr. Thaw, who had come to Pittsburgh as a banker, had a good business eye and for a time thought of buying and selling real estate. But he wrote in one of his letters, "As for speculation there is no chance, landed property being already monopolized by monied men & held at very high prices."

Pittsburgh in 1783 numbered "perhaps 60 wooden houses

and cabins" said Schoepf, "in which live something more than 100 families. . . . The first stone house was built this summer, but soon many good buildings may be seen, because the place reasonably expects to grow large and considerable with the passage of time." There were no houses of worship or justice, but only a resident German preacher; and the Pennsylvania government sent a judge once or twice a year to administer justice.

By 1796-97 a traveler named Baily mentioned that Pittsburgh houses were still mostly of wood, although lately people had begun to build them with brick. The streets did not always cross at right angles, but near the rivers they ran parallel with the stream. In 1802 the burgess and his assistants advertised in the *Pittsburgh Gazette* for bids for digging and walling with stone or brick four wells in Market Street, not less than forty-seven feet deep. A few months later pumps had been installed at two of these wells.

Pittsburgh had become, when Mr. Thaw arrived, the "western exchange," a reflex of New York, in its earnest bustle and in the same variety of thronging strangers. By 1807 Christian Schultz, another traveler who passed through on one of those western tours that were then becoming fashionable, said that the town contained many houses that would be called elegant even in New York.

The town grew so rapidly that five years later the first traffic regulations were necessary. Since streets easily became encumbered with wagons and drays, a fine of two dollars was to be collected by street commissioners from the owners of vehicles that were a nuisance. If these officers failed in their duty they themselves were fined from fifty cents to two dollars. And in winter sleighs could not be driven faster than a trot.

Town houses throughout western Pennsylvania had greatly improved over the first unhewn log structures. As early as the 1780's, weatherboarding had come into use, and houses built of such material, as well as houses of stone and brick, were two and even three stories high. Staircases had been built, and glass panes were usual for windows, which were few and small at first. When Mr. Thaw bought his home in Pittsburgh, Albert Gallatin had been making glass at New Geneva on the Monongahela River for eleven years. And for four years O'Hara and Craig had been making window glass on the south side of the Monongahela—glass which measured as much as eighteen by twenty-four inches.

Inside, the houses belonging to the more affluent classes had become more cheerful, lighter with the entrance of sun through glass panes and colorful with wall papers recently imported from the East. Against such walls gleamed sideboards and well turned, polished tables of cherry or walnut. Mr. Thaw wrote to his father back East:

"We have no mahogany here, but a cherry wood that looks nearly as well & plenty of Walnut. We have no difficulty in procureing Furniture of this at about the Philada prices & about double for crockery and glass ware with which & for the second time in so short a course of house keeping, am I now providing myself."

Glass and pewter lamps welcomed the incoming guest at night, and flowers from the well-kept garden brightened hallways and bedrooms. Fire irons of wrought iron or brass made the hearth cheerful. Bookcases with paneled or diamond-shaped glass panes held bound volumes stamped with gilt titles, and recent numbers of magazines, almanacs, and newspapers might be found on the table by the fireside. This was the age of objects eagerly sought today by collectors—of ladder back chairs and Seth Thomas clocks.

In town homes the housewife found life much more pleasant than the frontier farm woman had found it. Her household duties were less arduous. Her kitchen was equipped with utensils that any woman would be pleased with, articles with which she could make dainties for an ill member of her family or for those visitors who were now so much more frequent and with whom she could daily exchange kitchen and dining room secrets. The woman who had left a cultured life in the East, with its home conveniences, was no longer compelled to do back-breaking work in the truck patch and clearing and then to be satisfied with a bowl of mush and milk for supper, or with hog and hominy, and without dainties because she had neither ingredients nor utensils to make them. She could now, if she were fairly well off in the town, have a chafing dish, a muffineer, and a punch bowl. She could furnish her kitchen and table with glassware. Caddies and canisters of japanned tinware stood on the kitchen shelves and held beans, coffee, tea, and sugar.

Most kitchens had ovens and stoves with which women could cook in comfort, without singeing their hair, filling their eyes with smoke, and breaking their backs by leaning low over the hearth coals. It was not necessary now to bake corn cake in the ashes or on a clean ash board in front of the fire. There were ovens, often opening from outside the house, into which loaves, laid on grape leaves, were slid on a long paddle. Cannon stoves shaped like upright cylinders had come into use. Then the Franklin stoves and grates, as coal became plentiful, warmed the early parlors.

Where dining tables of cherry or walnut could not be afforded, the older type of table served, long boards three feet wide laid on trestles and covered with linen cloths or Holland huskaback. The old custom still prevailed of placing the salt-cellar, usually of pewter, in the middle of the table and covering it with a napkin. Sugar boxes or sugar pots and milk ewers were in use, although many families still used leather pitchers. Wooden jugs, waxed and bound and tipped with metal, made pouring convenient. Children were served their soft foods in porringers and posset cups.

After the Revolutionary War china generally replaced the earlier wooden trenchers. There were charming blue-edged plates that brightened the table, and yellow-flowered cups used without saucers at first and then with a deep saucer in which tea and coffee were poured to cool. Now forks were three-pronged, and—a great innovation had taken place—people actually used forks to carry food to the mouth instead of merely to hold meat while cutting it. But napkins were still badly needed, and every proud housewife had an abundant supply, as fingers were much used in eating.

Improvements in table service kept pace with the increase of delicacies. Old papers announce for sale at the stores of the day chocolate, spices of all kinds, red and sugar almonds, muscatel raisins, dried peas, and such luxuries as imported wines and liquors—Madeira, sherry, claret, Lisbon, and port wines, and

TEA KETTLE

French and Spanish brandies. Not only the town aristocracy now brought to their tables such dainties as spiced fruits, preserves, candied fruits and flowers, and marmalades; many housewives pickled purple cabbage with samphire and fennel, put up nasturtium buds, and candied elder flowers. They had sugar shears to cut the huge cones of loaf sugar that were bought wrapped in blue-purple paper. Curds and creams, tarts, trifles, floating islands, and whipped sillabubs, once great delicacies although they were not altogether unknown, were now common to many.

Meats and vegetables, sweets and pastries were all put on the table together, often with a "grand conceit" of fruits for center ornament. The average doctor's or lawyer's family, or the family of average means, frequently dined from a single abundant dish, a great round pewter dish heaped with a tasty stew, perhaps. Puddings were served before meat, so that visitors dropping in before the family had eaten were wont to say, "I came early, in pudding time." Town tables had become something more than a source of strength for frontier tasks. They were attractive gathering places and instruments of sociability.

Prices of foodstuffs, dry goods, and other common articles have survived in old papers and account books. From 1796 to 1800 a pound of sugar sold for thirty-five cents. A yard of calico cost a dollar and a quarter; a quarter pound of ginger, eighteen cents; the same weight of pepper, thirty cents; a bushel of salt, a dollar and thirty-five cents; and a pound of coffee, fifty-eight cents. An almanac cost twelve cents. A wool hat could be bought for two dollars and thirty-five cents. A half paper of pins was worth eighteen cents; an ounce of indigo sold for twenty-two cents. A ton of hay was worth six dollars; a scythe, a dollar and a half; and five pounds of nails, about one dollar.

Charming, old-fashioned gardens inclosed by box hedges, grew up about many of the homes—plots of pleasant confusion where flowers, herbs, and vegetables grew together and which, after rain, when the sun came out, filled the air with pungent fragrance. At the bottom of the gardens were planted gooseberry and currant bushes and quince and crab apple trees; the whole expanse was frequently below street level and was protected from hogs, dogs, and intruders by a paling fence. From such gardens ladies plucked sprigs of rosemary or southernwood to carry to church to sniff at, and they picked striped grasses to lay between leaves of their books. Here grew the sweet smelling lavender that they placed between sheets in the linen chest. Against the fence climbed hollyhocks, and over the paths sweetbriar trailed. Against the house walls were trellised apricots and peaches. Roses were gathered to make rose water for the toilet table and to lay among spices in rose jars. Peonies, yellow day lilies, clumps of iris, lilac bushes, squills, and syringa all helped to make the town gardens.

Herbs so necessary to the savory dishes that appeared on the supper table, to the preserving of fruits and candying of flowers, and for family ailments, were supplied from a little plot. Sage, anise, mint, balm, and herbs transplanted from fields beyond the edge of the town, such as pennyroyal and boneset, were grown here. Some housewives made "pin money" from seeds gathered in their gardens.

The garden was lived in, too. Early diaries and letters tell of day-to-day tasks carried out in a summer house, or on a garden bench. Ladies sat there to cast up their household accounts, or in apron, garden hat, and gloves to protect their hands from thorns and soil they worked among vines and shrubs. If a letter was to be answered, quill pen and sander were carried into the garden. Young mothers who taught their children their A B C's took children and books there, and if the lessons were well learned a tale might be read or told before some task or errand was set. In the shade of the summer house, where the sun could not reach their complexions but where the fragrance of thyme and lavender reached, young ladies perused the latest novel or tatted a lace collar. Here the banker and his client might walk before supper, or the town lawyer talk with his wife of the wisdom of ordering a new barrel of salt, or even confide what town talk he had learned from the gentlemen he had "been closeted with."

ELM

The distinction of classes among town dwellers that Mr. Thaw noticed meant that the frontier had prospered, that men had accumulated money and, with it, had imported luxuries from the East, or they had founded businesses and industries to supply such goods. Safety and leisure allowed this class of people, even in country towns, to enjoy objects and pastimes that had once been luxuries but had now become part of daily life.

Not all frontier people, however, had invested money in lands or in the founding of businesses. Business and industry developed one class of men who owned and promoted and another class composed of the men who performed the actual work in the shops and offices. Increasing settlement and com-

fort had allowed more men to turn their full time to professions, such as law, medicine, and the ministry. They opened
offices in town or in their homes, and from there made their
usual circuits into the outlying country. Even the population
of smaller towns divided itself into two classes: the business
and professional men and the mechanics. An economic and
social life of complex rights and privileges had developed; and
its outward signs were different habits of home building, dress,
behavior, and general amusement.

The mechanics and workmen became familiar sights about
the streets and rivers in their long, loose trousers of tow and
their short, tight-fitting sailors' jackets, or roundabouts, made
in winter of linsey and in summer of nankeen, dimity, or linen.

Towns also bred other classes of people. Business and industry brought in their wake men and women who were not
the most desirable citizens, hangers-on of prosperity. In towns
such as Brownsville, Uniontown, and Pittsburgh, where road-
ways and waterways brought in large numbers of transients,
it was natural that many poor and shiftless persons should stop
over. Swindlers and sharpers gathered in such towns to cheat
or wheedle a living out of the citizens. Beggars, tramps, even
lunatics, were also unwelcome sojourners.

But such was the free, give-and-take spirit of the growing
communities that men of many different types mingled at certain places and times for amusements. River boatmen, Irish
traders, loafers, sharpers, honest mechanics, and young dandies
met for jovial pastimes and rough diversions in taprooms and
inn yards, especially on Sundays and holidays, for bull baiting,
cockfighting, gaming, and boxing "to the death." Horse racing,

too, was popular. At Pittsburgh, each autumn for several days the town was noisy with racing crowds gathered from all the country around, for the Jockey Club had a race track at the extreme northeastern corner of the town about where the Fort Pitt Hotel now stands.

Town dwellers and country dwellers alike found their days less taken up with household industries. A single family need no longer plant its own truck patch and make the tools to work with, to grow its own flax and spin and weave it into cloth for dresses and jackets, or to tan its own leather and make its own shoepacks and shoes. Men and women had time now to think about ideas and to gather for simple amusements and friendly visits. Many evenings were spent in telling tales and in singing to the accompaniment of the violin, spinet, or dulcimer, in dancing and card games of whist and bezique. Taverns set rooms apart as ballrooms. In Pittsburgh, for instance, at the "Sign of the Green Tree" the assembly room was often gay with young ladies and army officers and young men who by day read law or medicine. In the ballrooms of the "General Butler" and "Sign of the Waggon" practicing balls were held by dancing masters, with a cotillion at seven, concluded with country dances. Dancing classes were held also over William Irwin's tavern and store, for ladies at three o'clock, for gentlemen at six.

Rich and gay fashions modeled on the eastern and European vogues made streets and ballrooms colorful. Closer contacts had been established by travel, and papers announced new fabrics and designs for sale in the shops. Fashionable ladies who danced the cotillion or attended the dancing classes did so in tamboured frocks and petticoats, in silk and cotton shawls, with wreaths and plumes in their hair, their feet gliding and stepping in kid and morocco slippers. In the summer the ladies carried elaborate parasols, and if the weather was bad or if they rode in from outside the town they wore a "weather skirt." Men wore sherry-vallies, or spatterdashes, to protect their gay breeches. Cocked hats gave way to soft or stiff hats with low square crowns and straight brims. "Ruffles without shirts!" wrote Tarleton Bates, a fashionable young man about town, "I had no idea there was any such thing until receipt of your letter." In concluding his letter, he joked with his friend, "Confine yourself to rations and 'live like a Frenchman' and even wear ruffles without shirts." But men wore stranger things than ruffles without shirts. They carried muffs in winter and wore great thumb rings, and at the beginning of the century high, tasseled boots were worn much both in military and civil circles.

BED WARMER

Young people could now take up the finer accomplishments of the fashionable world. They could receive instruction in French, as Tarleton Bates did for ten dollars a quarter, or could learn to play the violin or to sing an air to an accompaniment. The *Pittsburgh Gazette* on December 2, 1786, published a notice: "Wanted, a man who understands Vocal Music, and who can teach it with propriety; such a person will meet with good encouragement from the Inhabitants of Pittsburgh." A Mr. Tyler, a chorister from England, had early settled in the town and taught sacred and secular music. Mr. Tyler did not confine his teaching to Pittsburgh. Indeed, by the end of the century almost every community had a singing master who gathered the people together in houses or crossroad schools and churches and taught them not only what songs he knew but often to play the flute or the fiddle, and if some one owned a spinet he could, if he had had Mr. Tyler's training, gather a few pupils and teach them to play fashionable airs and waltzes and the sonatas of Mozart and Martini. A town like Pittsburgh soon passed the benighted, backwoods stage as people like Mr. Tyler, Miss Sophia Weidner, and Mr. Declary came here to settle. The *Gazette* announced on August 31, 1799, a vocal and instrumental concert by Miss Weidner and Mr. Declary in the assembly room at the "Sign of the Green Tree." But Pittsburgh could not yet support such people by their chosen profession alone; so Mr. Declary later opened a grocery and dry goods shop. At any rate he found the community congenial, and no doubt he relieved his days of handling packages of soap and flour over his counter by teaching music to the promising young ladies and young men.

The whole tone of living had changed by the time Mr. Thaw first placed his quill pen and sander on his counting table at the bank. Settlements took off the rough edges of frontier character, and living together had made life more pleasant. In spite of the scarcity of churches and schools, people learned from one another, and the discipline acquired through frontier life had given mental and moral training, had improved people's manners, and had refined their tastes. If we add up all the items in the general life of the people who lived in the many towns scattered over western Pennsylvania at the close of the pioneer period, we should find the beginnings of a very genuine culture.

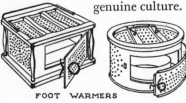

FOOT WARMERS

Meadville, set off more or less by itself in Crawford County, without easy contact with such an active town as Pittsburgh, had a number of citizens of intelligence and refinement. Its distance from other towns and its limited opportunities for reading and study led the inhabitants of the town to establish a public library of several hundred books on history, travel, biography, and the arts. In 1805 the Meadville Academy was chartered, later to become Allegheny College. At Washington, too, young men could attend the Washington Academy as early as 1789.

Much of the culture of the times found its expression in clubs of men gathered together to discuss and experiment in those fields in which they were interested. The Western Medical Society at Washington had members in Pittsburgh who found attending meetings at Washington so difficult that they organized their own Pittsburgh Medical Society. The young gentlemen of the town also had organized into an amateur theatrical club the year before Mr. Thaw came to the city. Their first performance, a popular comic opera, *The Poor Soldier,* was presented in the courthouse. A group of young men in Washington, Pennsylvania, had offered there a performance of Thomson's tragedy, *Tancred and Sigismunda,* and a curtain raiser in the form of a farce called *The Register.*

Town life made printing and distribution of newspaper and almanacs comparatively general. By 1805 a dozen papers and half a dozen almanacs were in circulation throughout western Pennsylvania from Erie to Uniontown. The early newspapers were printed on double sheets about half the size of present-day papers and sold for about six pence. Payment for subscriptions was taken in farm produce or merchandise when cash was not convenient. The papers were regularly delivered in towns, but in the country they were distributed more or less irregularly. Papers came into the district from as far away as Philadelphia and New York. The *Pittsburgh Gazette* made its appearance on July 29, 1786, and until 1795 was the only paper printed in western Pennsylvania. In that year the *Western Telegraphe and Washington Advertiser* was started in Washington, and in 1798 the *Fayette Gazette, and Union Advertiser* appeared at Uniontown. In 1799 the *Farmers Register* was begun in Greensburg. The northwestern section, too, had its papers— at Erie the *Mirror,* begun in 1808, and at Meadville the *Crawford Weekly Messenger,* begun in 1805. These early papers gave much space to the doings of the federal government and also to foreign correspondence, so that the settlers were in touch with general world affairs. Very little space, however, was devoted to local events, with the exception of politics.

Almanacs had been issued as early as 1788 by the *Gazette.* Zadok Cramer began publishing his famous series of almanacs about 1801; they contained receipts and prescriptions, astronomical calculations for Ohio, Virginia, and Kentucky, and selections from English writers. About the same time he issued the *Navigator,* a manual of information for voyagers on the western rivers. Cramer was an important figure in the development of literary life in the Pittsburgh district. He established in 1801 the first successful circulating library in Pittsburgh, which in time grew to contain about one thousand volumes. It was open three days a week to readers, on Monday, Wednesday, and Friday. Subscribers paid a dollar a month, two dollars for three months, two dollars and fifty cents for six months, and five dollars for the year. It was, however, at the print shop of the *Pittsburgh Gazette* that the first book written and printed west of the Allegheny Mountains, the third volume of Hugh Henry Brackenridge's *Modern Chivalry,* was issued in 1793.

Little by little life was taking on brighter colors, and slowly a grace of living was taking form. There were still hardships and privation and struggle with men and nature, plenty of ugliness, and in places much darkness of spirit and distortion of human lives out of their normal patterns. But there was a growth of lightness of spirit, if only at times and in scattered places.

OAK

The First Factories

XVI

AS INDUSTRIES expanded beyond the household, the aspect of the country and of towns changed rapidly. The frontier, in passing, had prepared the way for the growth of industry in shops and factories throughout the region. Early settlers had located coal and iron veins, had learned where salt could be found and where the best stone could be quarried. They had found good soil for bricks and pottery, and sand for making glass. Brickmaking developed rapidly in the 1790's; it was probably the first industry established in Pittsburgh, for there had been brickmakers with General Stanwix in 1759. And in 1789 John Ormsby advertised for rent a brick kiln on the south side of the Monongahela River. Weaving was passing out of the cabin and the home. In 1800 four looms were operating in Pittsburgh. By 1804 the first factory in Pittsburgh for carding, spinning, and weaving cotton yarns and materials was established by Peter Eltonhead, a cotton manufacturer from England. By 1809 forty-four weavers had opened establishments in the city. Cabinetmaking and upholstering were in progress in 1785. In the following year Hugh Ross opened a rope-making establishment. Hat and cap-making were carried on in 1786 to the extent of forty-two thousand hats yearly in four counties west of the Alleghenies. By 1799 the boot and shoemaking industry was well established. Saddlers and furriers prospered in towns on the main roads of travel.

More important than all these to the future of the region that was fast losing its pioneer character was the iron industry, which, in the early years of the nineteenth century, was already blackening the air over Pittsburgh. Step by step with the iron industry grew its brother industry, coal mining. As early as 1761 James Kenny had recorded in his journal that he had gone with four men from Fort Pitt to the mountain on the south side of the Monongahela, about one and a quarter miles from the river, and had brought home at night in a flatboat about forty bushels of fine coal.

The Penns in 1784 had granted permission to dig coal on certain lots, at a fixed price, as far in as the perpendicular line falling from the summit of the hill thereon. And when John Canon laid out Canonsburg, each purchaser was granted the right to mine coal on his own premises. After John Hayden had made the first iron west of the mountains in a blacksmith shop in 1790 the two industries grew together. Furnaces and forges were put into operation in a dozen sections of the region in as many years—Fairfield Furnace near Uniontown; Laurel Furnace on Laurel Run; Redstone Furnace, also near Uniontown; Springhill, Mary Ann, and Pine Grove Furnaces—by 1805 four furnaces and six forges were going in Fayette County. From such furnaces and forges the settlers, both those who lived in the district and those who were venturing through on their way down the Ohio, were supplied with pots, skillets,

BLAST FURNACE

grates, stoves, and castings of various kinds. Among the names of the founders of the steel empire that grew out of these early pioneer industries are those of William Turnbull and Peter Marmie, who built the Alliance Iron Works on Jacobs Creek in Fayette County; Isaac Meason, who constructed a furnace on Dunbar Creek four miles south of Connellsville; and George Anshutz, who set up in Pittsburgh the first furnace for smelting iron ore.

In some sections there grew up about these industries fair-sized iron plantations of several hundred acres, on which stood the mansion house of the owner, the furnace and forges, the charcoal house, the office, the store, the gristmill and the saw-mill, the blacksmith shop, and the common bake oven. There were also the barns, grain fields, and orchards, and the log cabins and houses of the workers. Plantations of note in western Pennsylvania were those of two early ironmasters: Nathaniel Gibson, who built, at Little Falls, Fayette County, one of the first large mansion houses in the Monongahela country before 1800; and Henry William Stiegel, who at about the same time set up a similar establishment at Elizabeth.

Until 1807 no steam engines were used in the industries of the region. In 1803, however, Oliver Evans had begun the making of steam engines in Philadelphia. It was he who built the first engine used in Pittsburgh, which was designed to run the gristmill of his son George at Water Street and Redoubt Alley. The mill was ready to grind meal in 1809 and was the first steam-driven factory in Pennsylvania west of the mountains. The engine that ran George Evans' gristmill announced the end of that era in western Pennsylvania that we call the pioneer period—the period during which trade and travel, education and religion, and art and science were in their crudest form—and it also announced the beginning of an era during which there developed a new way of living, new problems, new types of people, and new ideas. As the frontier passed into the Middle West, the towns it left behind along the Allegheny and Monongahela rivers changed their aspect and character as at the touch of Aladdin's lamp.

The *Pittsburgh Gazette,* which untiringly preached the advantages of the district to business men and farmers alike, carried in its pages in April, 1789, the following paragraph extolling the benefits of the region to mechanics and laborers:

HATTER'S BLOCK
AND MALLET

"This country offers at present the most unbounded encouragement to the artificer and labourer. . . . The reward which the mechanic meets with is greater than at any former period. One pair of shoes which costs 11s. 3d. will buy 180 lb. of wheat, which will furnish 120 lb. of flour; the shoes will also procure more than 60 lb. of good beef or pork. The necessaries of life are uncommonly low, and the workmanship of the industrious artisan, whether shoemaker, carpenter, taylor, or smith, is most amply and deservedly rewarded. We want people, we want sober and diligent tradesmen; hatters, button makers, rope makers, weavers, &c, will be more welcome, and will essentially promote our prosperity. We should employ our own workmen rather than foreigners, those of our own town or county in preference to those at a distance from us. I wish this state would give a bounty of forty shillings to every mechanic or labourer who arrives in it from Europe. Population and industry are the true causes of national greatness."

In towns throughout western Pennsylvania a class of laborers and mechanics rapidly developed. Streets resounded with sounds of hammers on anvils, and of saws in carpenters' shops and cabinetmakers' establishments. Shoemakers were busy at their lasts. Saddlers astride their benches stitched industriously. Tailors sat cross-legged to make breeches, an important trade in itself for many years. Soap and candle works, dye works, and machine works grew from month to month, and with them grew the class of artisans who ran them. Towns were likewise centers from which journeymen could travel through the country; itinerant coopers, gunsmiths, ironworkers, and weavers found a great deal of work in the back country.

THUMB
LATCH

Skilled labor soon became plentiful, but unskilled labor was scarce. In 1804 a tin factory in Pittsburgh employed twenty-eight persons, a nail factory thirty persons, and a cotton manufactory twelve persons; thirty workmen were employed in shipbuilding, about fifty in boat building, and thirty in the ropewalks. Large numbers of boys were apprenticed at very early ages to practically every trade. Such apprentices were in general humanely treated, for they were under the protection of the state. In 1789 a certain Patrick Flynn, aged eighteen, was apprenticed to dwell with and serve Hugh Ross for three years, during which time he was to be taught the art and mystery of rope-making and to be given each winter three months' evening schooling. William Maloney, aged ten years, was apprenticed in 1796 to a farmer in Fayette County under the usual terms. He was to serve his master ten years "in all lawful and reasonable service." His master, in turn, was to provide "sufficient meat, drink, apparel, washing, and lodging"; was to teach or cause him to be taught "the art, trade or mystery of a farmer"; and was to give him two years' schooling in reading, writing, and arithmetic. At the expiration of the boy's term the master was to give him "two complete suits of Apparel, one of which to be new."

Slavery took root in the western counties and lasted longer there than anywhere else in Pennsylvania. Although the typical frontiersman had a natural dislike for slavery and, moreover, could not afford to keep slaves, and although slaves were not ordinarily profitable in western Pennsylvania except as domestic servants in well-to-do families, yet there were recorded in 1792 in Allegheny, Washington, Westmoreland, and Fayette counties 878 slaves, or one to every eighty-seven persons. A slave woman sold for about one thousand dollars in Fayette County in 1794, and it was said that this price was representative. The statement has been made that six of the early ministers in and around Pittsburgh and nearly all the elders and church officers were slave owners. H. H. Brackenridge said in his *Modern Chivalry* that many men in the district who "would not for a fine cow have shaved their beards on a Sunday" held and abused slaves. They were bartered for cattle or farm produce. They were exposed to public sale: "Horses, cows, sheep, stills, negroes, and household furniture." A farm of 360 acres was advertised for sale in the *Gazette* on February 2, 1790, the terms of payment to be half in cash and the balance in negroes. Slaves were often sold at public outcry in the streets of Greensburg.

In 1780 a state law declared that all negroes and mulattoes born of slave mothers should become free after they reached the age of twenty-eight. But the law was not effective. In 1788 a law decreed that all slaves brought into the state should be immediately freed. As late as 1840, however, some slaves were still held in western Pennsylvania, and in 1845 one is recorded in Washington County.

More profitable to trade and industry in western Pennsylvania than slaves, however, were the indentured servants and apprentices and the workmen who were paid daily or weekly wages. In the 1750's the highest wage paid to ironworkers was eighty-four cents a day, but after the Revolutionary War workers were scarce, and wages advanced. One ironworks advertised for furnace men and offered wages of twelve dollars a week with board and lodging and whiskey every day. In the 1790's twenty to forty cents a day was fair pay for a day's work. By 1809 ordinary workmen were paid from sixty-seven cents to one dollar a day, and this was said by one observer to be more in proportion than in any other region because of the low cost of living in Pittsburgh. Most accounts, nevertheless, mention that living was high in Pittsburgh. John Thaw was of such opinion. If a business man of Mr. Thaw's standing and means found prices high, the mechanics and tradesmen must also have found them so. In 1786 the advertisement in the *Gazette* of Daniel Britt and Company showed that although furs and peltry were no longer used as money, goods were still exchanged by barter. Daniel Britt and Company announced that they had for sale a general allotment of merchandise, "which will be sold on reasonable terms for cash, flour, whiskey, beef, pork, bacon, wheat, rye, oats, corn, ashes, candle wick, tallow, etc. etc. etc." A young man who had been given a piece of land—two hundred acres—sold it to a man in the neighborhood for "a cow and calf and a wool hat."

Money was still in a confused state in the 1790's. The earliest settlers had brought little money with them to the frontier, and only those who were close to shipping points and who worked farms large enough to produce a surplus for shipping could sell their crops or stock. Currency was never stable. During the Revolution this confusion in currency was made worse for a time by the introduction of Continental money, which had depreciated in value, and also by the introduction of Virginia money and money from New York. English, French, and Spanish coins were brought north from the New Orleans market and sometimes found their way to the East in return for goods purchased there. Business accounts preserved from those days show that English currency predominated even after the federal government began to coin money in 1792. United States currency, or for that matter, any currency, was scarce in the western country until after the establishment of the first bank in 1804. Until that time banking had been done for the settler by a lawyer, a friend, a post rider, or a pack-horse driver who happened to be going to Philadelphia.

Until after the Whiskey Insurrection of 1794 whiskey was the chief circulating medium, the money of the western country. A gallon of good rye whiskey at any store in the district and at every farmhouse in southwestern Pennsylvania was the equal of a shilling coin. An early historian says that two barrels of whiskey would buy a good corner lot. But the pages of the *Pittsburgh Gazette* show that bonds, bank certificates, drafts, and promissory notes were in fairly wide circulation.

Industry and trade, however, increased the need for coins and for the establishment of banks to handle the commercial notes and the credit of merchants and manufacturers. Financial organization of this kind meant that the workingmen could put the large copper cents, the quarters, and the occasional half dollars into the pockets of their tow trousers or jeans. But most people who carried money about did not for a long time carry many American coins. More likely they carried the "levy" or eleven-penny bit, the commonest coin in circulation, equal to one-eighth of a dollar. The fivepenny bit, fippeny bit, or "fip," which was the Spanish half-real, was sometimes called by the name given it in Louisiana, the picayune. If a man were well off he might have some pieces of eight in his purse. These coins of pirate fame were the original Spanish dollar, after which the first silver dollars coined by the United States mint were modeled. They were, after the Revolution, the standard unit of money. A piece, or dollar, was worth eight reals; hence the name pieces of eight. Sometimes a Spanish dollar was cut into quarters or eighths with a chisel, and the smaller division was known as "a bit." Besides these, French money, chiefly the napoleon, was in wide circulation. Every man had almost to be a banker to transact business in the currency of those days. The almanacs of the day printed tables to help compute values of one coin in terms of another. And this condition lasted for some years after the beginning of the nineteenth century.

With high prices and the complicated system of money, the common laborer found life none too easy. Labor or trade unions developed slowly, and were in a primitive state until the middle of the nineteenth century. A few trade societies had

BELLOWS

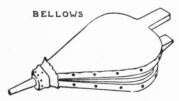

been organized, however—one in Pittsburgh in 1788 and another in Washington, Pennsylvania. These were intended to educate the working people, to induce them to settle in towns, and thus to attract manufacturers. Membership was not restricted to members of one trade, but was open to all workers in the town who wished to join. These societies paid no attention to wages or working conditions. They were, until the end of the 1790's, rather in the nature of guilds or social groups. But in 1804 the journeymen shoemakers in Pittsburgh found their wages insufficient in proportion to the cost of living. When the price of board was raised and wages remained stationary, these journeymen shoemakers issued the following statement:

"Pittsburgh, December 19, 1804. This notice is intended to inform the traveling journeymen shoemakers of Pennsylvania, or of any other State, that the journeymen of this town made a turnout for higher wages. Two or three of their employers had a meeting, and having a number of apprentices thought proper to advise the other master shoemakers to raise the boarding from $1.50 to $2.25 per week. We think it our duty to give this notice to all journeymen shoemakers that they may be guarded against imposition. The following are the prices which we turned out for, viz.: Fine shoes, 80 cents; coarse shoes, 75 cents; women's slippers, 75 cents; boottees, $2.00; long boots, $2.50; cossacks, $2.50; N. B. We would not advise any journeymen to come here unless they want a seat of cobbling."

This was probably the first strike in Pittsburgh. It meant that the day had passed when the ordinary migrant to the West struggled alone to gain a living on his frontier farm. It meant that agriculture and stock-raising were no longer the chief means of living. It meant that the early wilderness of the western region had been transformed into progressive communities. It meant that the foundations of the future industrial empire had been laid.

The declaration of the journeymen shoemakers was a dramatic moment, for it marked a stage in the march of a gigantic army that was moving ever westward in the conquest of forests and savagery. In each stage of this march a higher level of living had been established. There had come first the hardy scouts, the traders, trappers, hunters, and military adventurers. These had passed through a state of semi-civilization in which they had learned from the savages themselves the means of coping with savagery. By these means and through their own resources they blazed the wilderness for the oncoming settlers.

Then up the main streams and water courses and over the almost roadless mountains came hardy bands of pioneers, the main body of the army, battling at every step against natural dangers and against the perils of warfare, illness, and solitude. Once having gained a foothold in an isolated clearing or a small community, the first farmers were reënforced by stock-raisers and herdsmen who brought droves of cattle, hogs, sheep, and horses over well-worn trails and half-formed roads. Each settler defended his home for himself—against the dangers of the wilderness and against other claimants who threatened his rights. As settlement increased, however, safety was found in numbers and disputes over land ownership grew less frequent. Then this growing army of pioneers, who had won their lands through bitter contest, both with the rival French claimants

BLACKSMITH SHOP

and with the native savages, finally won the right to establish their own institutions independent of the mother country from which most of them had come.

With peaceful possession insured, the last frontier stage began. The settlers now took up new tasks; and to aid the farmer and the stock-raiser came the tradesman and the mechanic. Ever increasing numbers invaded the western Pennsylvania country and swept beyond it to reproduce in new places the process of pioneering. Those who held fast to the lands that had already been won were eager now to improve their ways of life. From the soil they had once cleared of forests and from which their farms had been won, on which their stock had been nourished, and on which their towns had been built, they now drew treasures of materials as the basis for a new empire. Deeper under the surface than the seeds they planted lay valuable ores and veins of coal. And in the streams that flowed through this soil was power to convert these materials to their own uses.

The initial work was over. The first great advance was accomplished. With the increase of craftsmen and laborers, the servants of growing industry; with the ring of hammers, the hum of saws, the rattle of wheels over cobbles, and the drifting of factory smoke through the air; with the clamor of forges and the hiss of the steam engines that drove them, pioneering was at an end. The onetime frontier had become history.

The Road to the Past

XVII

THE past is always with us. We may never think or care at all about it, but there it is for good or bad, guiding and controlling us in every thought and act. Since time began men and women had wondered about the past, told tales about it, tales of courage and heroism that stir and move us, and they have tried for many reasons and by many means to recapture it.

To discover the truth about the past takes long and careful searching. Much useless, tasteless, and harmful material obscures the road that the reader or student must follow if he seeks a past that is real. If he wishes to find that historical land from which he came, born of its traditions and its shadowy thoughts and customs, he must choose his way with judgment. Otherwise he will become lost in hazy impressions that will serve only to cloud his mind.

Among the accounts and records of the times and places in which we had our beginning, much is true and valuable; much is false and misleading. Those who have given time and thought to the study of history have learned what materials they can best trust and what is unreliable. In reconstructing the past they have divided these materials into two classes:

primary materials, the true sources of information, which are "usually the by-products of the actual business of living, back of which the scholar cannot go in his search for new facts and truths"; and *secondary* materials. Primary materials include such things as objects, letters, diaries, and newspaper accounts nearest to the times and conditions we want to recapture. Secondary works deal with times and conditions at second-hand; they are writings *based* on data that actually survive from the period.

Relics, or remnants, are perhaps the most primary of all sources. The cabin that has been left standing, if it has not been remodeled; the candle molds that have lain in the old loft or attic; the pewter dishes that have been hidden in some dark cupboard or in the rafters where the hands that last used them put them one day years ago—these are relics that have survived and are actual, visible tokens of life long past. Many such articles have been collected and placed in museums or have been cleaned and put out to decorate a shelf or modern fireplace. Here and there they may yet be found in less traveled districts, in barns or attics, or in the more backward mountain places where they are still in use by persons who frequently do not know where the relics came from. Some of these relics have always been in the house and have been used since anyone in the family can remember.

Old things have a way of establishing themselves in the lives of those who use them for a long time, especially if they are soundly made to begin with, as most of the old tools and utensils were. Careful workmanship was customary in the past, and cheap substitutes for good materials were rare. The old-fashioned furniture displayed in antique shops along the highways, although often reworked and repaired, are relics of past tastes and ways of living. Since such things do not always survive in their first, most authentic state, they are of varying degrees of accuracy. Sketches and paintings of places and persons and objects are also primary material. But these especially vary in point of accuracy. Pictures, as we know, may not reveal the true design, even when they are photographs. How much less reliable is a drawing likely to be, in which the judgment and ability of the artist may or may not have been equal to the task. Nevertheless, sketches of early Pittsburgh and of the first courthouse at Greensburg help to give us some ideas of the towns and buildings of the past. Old newspapers show us the

TIN LANTERN state of printing and of advertising and tell us when certain luxuries and conveniences were first introduced. Old books show us much about papermaking and applied arts such as bookbinding and decorating, and show us, too, what words people used and how they handled words and ideas.

Diaries and journals of early ministers, traders, travelers, and army officers are invaluable sources of history, although these also differ in their degrees of value. A diary kept during a trip into the westward lands, for instance, is better source material than a journal written after the trip. The diaries of certain early preachers in western Pennsylvania re-create for us the ways of travel, the life and customs of the people in the settlements, the way in which early church services were held, and many other details, which put together in their proper relationship build up chapters in books. The diary of James Kenny, Indian trader at Fort Pitt, tells us about early trade, planting, and the first coal dug from the hills along the Monongahela; about the floods at the Point, and the fires that broke out in the cabins and storehouses.

Minutes of church meetings and of political caucuses, of conventions and trade meetings, account books of early merchants, and the account books of farmers who recorded their transactions and the wages they paid their helpers are all historical sources of great importance.

Much of the written material is difficult to find when it is needed. Transcripts have therefore been made by students who have already used the old documents, letters, and manuscripts; these transcripts are accurately typed copies that can be kept in convenient places for study. They are valuable because they make such records available to larger numbers of persons than could reach the originals, and the copies save the originals from overuse or careless use and thus help to preserve them. One collection of transcripts covers the records of fourteen Presbyterian churches in southwestern Pennsylvania, records of sessions and congregational meetings, of preachers' baptismal registers and such things.

Many a pleasant summer afternoon can be spent over such records in an old church in the country, while bees buzz about the open windows and a cardinal sings in the elms outside. Or winter afternoons can be spent in a musty courthouse in one of the smaller towns, when the shadows are growing in the corners and the lights outside grow bright on the snow. There is no better lesson in history than to search out these records and to pore over them ourselves, or to visit the museums and historical societies and see what a flail is, to handle the old guns and hackles actually used by hands that have long been dust.

Besides these sources, there are interesting old-fashioned books, weather-stained and broken-backed, written by persons who lived through most of the events they describe. They have told us how they built their cabins, defended their forts, worked in their fields, made merry at the fulling bees, what they sang and read, what they ate and wore, and what they thought of and dreamed of in the days that are no longer dead to us as we read and relive the vividly recorded experiences.

Regional histories are histories written about a particular district that has been important as a geographic, political, or economic entity. The early accounts of western Pennsylvania are reliable within limitations. Their authors often lacked primary data on which to base judgments and statements of fact. And they were usually not trained in the procedure of historical method. Too often a faulty memory or inaccurate accounts and tales of their times by old survivors, or inaccurate earlier written accounts formed their guides. Nevertheless such books inevitably show some of the personality of the authors, and from their pages we gather the sense and atmosphere of times past, which is the most elusive thing the historian has to capture, the final grace of all historical writing, and without which such writing is as dead as the bones of the horses that plowed the fields of the pioneers. Such books have a definite value because frequently they offer the first organized, synthesized information about incidents and regions, which we should not have had if these pleasant antiquarians had not written it down for us.

Finally, there are stories, poems, essays, and plays that rebuild and illumine the past for us, many of them with truth and beauty.

The authors would like to mention here a few of the books to which the interested student may refer for additional reading in connection with western Pennsylvania history. For an entertaining and concise account of practically every phase of early pioneer life, there is Joseph Doddridge's *Notes on the Settlement and Indian Wars of the Western Parts of Virginia and Pennsylvania from 1763 to 1783*. Another chronicle of the pioneer period is James Veech's *The Monongahela of Old*.

The *Diary* of the Reverend David McClure records something of the manners and religion of the western Pennsylvania frontier people. Joseph Smith's *Old Redstone; or, Historical Sketches of Western Presbyterianism* is also valuable for its insight into early churches, missionaries, and ministers.

Fort Pitt and Letters from the Frontier, compiled by Mary C. Darlington, contains the journals of Céloron de Blainville and Captain William Trent (the journal of the latter is erroneously ascribed to Simeon Ecuyer) and numerous letters concerning Indian campaigns before 1800. The report of the Indian Forts Commission of Pennsylvania on the *Frontier Forts of Pennsylvania* gives locations and descriptions and contains many excellent maps, plans, and illustrations.

Two other books that should not be overlooked are Charles W. Dahlinger's *Pittsburgh: A Sketch of Its Early Social Life,* which depicts the political and social life of Pittsburgh early in its transition from wilderness town to metropolis; and Frank Cowan's *Southwestern Pennsylvania in Song and Story.*

The works of Henry W. Shoemaker are especially valuable

for the way in which his retelling of old time stories and legends has re-created the past. He is also the author of several interesting and useful books on the wild animals of Pennsylvania.

Among the most authoritative and interesting of the secondary works dealing with the history of Pennsylvania during the pioneer period are the several books written by C. Hale Sipe, and they will prove useful to any one looking for sketches of individual pioneers and Indian chiefs. Clarence E. McCartney's *Not Far from Pittsburgh,* and *Right Here in Pittsburgh,* should also be mentioned.

The other books in the series of which this volume is one are John Harpster's *Pen Pictures of Early Western Pennsylvania,* a collection of travelers' accounts; Russell J. Ferguson's *Early Western Pennsylvania Politics;* Leland D. Baldwin's *Pittsburgh: The Story of a City,* and *Whiskey Rebels: The Story of a Frontier Uprising;* Solon J. Buck's and Elizabeth H. Buck's *The Planting of Civilization in Western Pennsylvania; With Rifle and Plow: Stories of the Western Pennsylvania Frontier* by J. E. Wright, Elisabeth M. Sellers, and Jeanette C. Shirk; and *Guidebook to Historic Places in Western Pennsylvania.* Books yet to be issued in the series are: Randolph C. Downes, *Indian Affairs in the Upper Ohio Valley;* E. Douglas Branch, *Travelways of Western Pennsylvania;* Arthur Pound, *Two Centuries of Industry;* and Leland D. Baldwin, *The Keelboat Age on Western Waters.*

In the field of fiction, the following are highly entertaining stories aside from their value in presenting clear pictures of particular phases: Henry C. McCook, *The Latimers: A Tale of the Western Insurrection of 1794;* Andrew L. Russell, *The*

Freighter: A Tale of the Pittsburgh Frontier; and Richard T. Wiley, *Sim Greene and Tom the Tinker's Men: A Narrative of the Whisky Insurrection.*

A satirical novel in Don Quixote trend is Hugh H. Brackenridge's *Modern Chivalry: Containing the Adventures of a Captain, and Teague O'Regan, His Servant.* It casts much light upon life in western Pennsylvania at the end of the eighteenth century and contains, as well, the political sentiments of the famous Brackenridge. *Old Fort Duquesne: or, Captain Jack, the Scout,* by Charles McKnight, is heartily recommended for its color and treatment of the early days in the upper Ohio Valley. More recently written novels are *The Judas Tree,* by Neil H. Swanson, which deals with the frontier in the days of Pontiac's conspiracy and offers an extensive portrayal of the siege of Fort Pitt; *The First Rebel,* by the same author, based upon the actual adventures of James Smith as an Indian captive, and of the Black Boys' resistance to British tyranny several years before the Revolution; and Mary Schumann's *Strife Before Dawn,* a tale of Pittsburgh during the Indian Wars and the Revolution. Two fine children's stories recently published are *Moccasins in the Wilderness,* and *Rifles Beyond Fort Pitt,* both by Elizabeth H. Buck.

These are only a part of the books to which we can go for a very full and readable account of old days in the hills of western Pennsylvania, days that have left only their memory and their shadows. But the memory and the shadows are around us still, whether we move in and out of them with eyes unseeing or whether we pause to be charmed with their shapes and colors, trying to hold them for a moment before they dissolve.

Glossary

GLOSSARY

APPLE BUTTER "BILIN' "—*See* p. 111

BARLOW KNIFE—A one-bladed jackknife.

BARRACK—A large structure or row of buildings for lodging soldiers or workmen.

BARTER—To trade by exchanging goods for other goods without using money.

BASTION—*See* p. 118

BELTZNICKEL MAN—*See* p. 90

BETTY LAMP—*See* p. 49

BEZIQUE—Played with a deck of 64 cards and similar to pinochle.

BLACK MAN'S BASE—Also called BLACK MAN'S TIG. A long rope is tied to a gate or pole and one of the players holds the end of the rope and tries to catch another player. When he succeeds in doing so, the one captured joins him by holding hands and helps to catch the other players. The game is finished when all the players are caught.

BOHEA—A black tea of an inferior quality, so named from the hills on which it grows in China.

BRAZIER—A pan for holding hot coals.

BUTTING POLE—*See* p. 46

CADDY—A small box or can for holding tea, etc.

CALK—To drive filling into the seams between logs or planks, or to stop up the crevices.

CANDLE DIP—*See* p. 49

CANDLE MOLD—*See* pp. 49 and 81

CANDLEWOOD—*See* p. 48

CANISTER—A box or small container, usually of metal for holding tea, coffee, etc.

CASEMATE—A shelter of stone in which cannons are kept. There are small openings through which they can be fired.

CEDARWARE—*See* p. 53

CHAIN—In weaving, each stitch is dependent upon the preceding one.

CHEESE HOOP—A broad hoop or cylinder, usually of wood in which curd is pressed in making cheese.

CHICORY—A plant with bright blue flowers. Its leaves are used for salad; its roots are roasted and used as a substitute for coffee.

CHIPPED LOG—A log which has had the bark removed.

CLAPBOARD—A narrow board often thicker at one edge than the other, used for covering the outer walls of frame buildings.

COCKLOFT—An upper loft or attic; a smaller garret next to the roof.

CONCH-SHELL—A large spiral sea shell often converted into a horn.

COONSKIN—The skin of a raccoon used as material for caps.

COOPER—To make or repair casks, barrels, tubs, and other containers made of staves held together by hoops.

COPPERAS—A green chemical used in dyeing and in making inks.

CORDELLE—A towline or towrope.

CORNSTALK FIDDLE—A fiddle whittled from a cornstalk.

COW-CABBAGE—An inferior kind of cabbage.

COWLE—A large tub for holding water.

DAUB—To coat or cover with plaster, clay, mud, etc.

DELFTWARE—A kind of brown pottery covered with a solid white glaze over which a decoration is often painted. It was first made in the town of Delft, Holland.

DISTAFF—A split stick about a yard long, used for holding a bunch of flax, tow or wool from which thread is drawn in spinning yarn.

DRAWBRIDGE—A bridge which may be entirely or partly lifted, lowered, or moved aside.

DULCIMER—A musical instrument with wire strings, played with two light hammers.

ELECAMPANE—A large plant with yellow flowers. The root was used in the treatment of lung disorders.

ERYSIPELAS—An acute infectious disease that causes fever and a deep-red inflammation of the skin.

EWER—A wide-mouthed pitcher or jug for holding water or milk.

FILLING—Usually anything of an inferior quality introduced to increase bulk, especially in weaving.

FIRKIN—A small wooden cask for holding butter or lard. A firkin of butter weighs about 56 pounds.

FLAIL—*See* p. 66

FLATBOAT—A boxlike boat much used for downstream transportation on the western rivers. *See* p. 189

FLINT—A very hard black stone that strikes fire with steel.

FLITCH—A side of bacon, or the cured side of any animal.

FORD—The place where a river, stream, or other body of water is not too deep to cross by walking through the water.

FOX AND GEESE—Seventeen engraved pieces called geese are placed in an order similar to chess; the objective of the game is to corner the odd piece called the fox.

FREEBOOTER—A pirate, or buccaneer.

FROW—A cleaving tool used in splitting logs.

FULLED—*See* p. 77

FULLING BEE—*See* p. 111

GARRISON—A fortified place in which soldiers are stationed.

GIRDLE—To make a circular cut around a tree, through the bark and cortex, and thus to kill the tree.

GOOSE YOKE—A frame worn on the neck of an animal to prevent its passing through a fence or hedge. *See* p. 69

GOURD—A vegetable related to the pumpkin. Its dried skin was used for bowls, pitchers, etc.

GRIDIRON—An iron utensil with parallel bars used for broiling over a fire.

GUILD—The union of men in one trade to keep standards high and to look out for the interests of their trade.

HACKLE—*See* pp. 76 and 77

HAFT—A handle, as of a cutting tool; especially of an ax.

HALF-FACED CAMP—*See* p. 19

HAME—One of two curved pieces of wood to which traces are fastened; used in heavy draft.

HAND MILL—*See* p. 75

HASP—A hinged metal clasp for a door or a box which folds over a staple and is fastened with a pin or padlock.

HAYCOCK—A heap of hay shaped like a cone.

HEADRIGHT SYSTEM—*See* p. 31

HELVE—*See* p. 87

HEWED LOG CABIN—A cabin of logs roughly squared with an ax.

HOG YOKE—*See* goose yoke.

HORNBEAM—A tree which has a smooth gray bark and hard white wood; the leaves resemble those of a beech tree.

HORNBOOK—*See* p. 95

HOUSE RAISING—*See* p. 45

HURLY-BURLY—*See* p. 104

HYSON SKIN—A Chinese green tea having a special twist.

JACK—A small pitcher or drinking cup made of waxed leather coated on the outside with tar or pitch.

JACOBITE—A term applied to the period in which James II of England lived. It was about 1690 A.D.

JAMB—One of the side pieces of a window, door, or fireplace.

JEAN—Twilled cotton cloth used for overalls.

JERK—Meat that has been dried by cutting it in slices and exposing it to the sun.

JIGGING—Dancing a jig, a lively dance.

JOHNNYCAKE—A flat cake of corn meal mixed with milk or water, eggs, etc., and baked.

JOIST—One of the parallel pieces of timber to which the boards of a floor or ceiling are fastened.

KEELBOAT—A long, thin keel-bottomed boat propelled by poles or oars used on the western rivers for both downstream and upstream transportation. *See* p. 191

KEELER—A broad, shallow tub, used for holding milk or for washing dishes.

LATCHSTRING—*See* p. 43

LEAGUE—A measure of distance, usually about 3 miles.

LEEK—An onionlike plant used as food or flavoring.

LEEWARD—The side away from the wind.

LINSEY—A shortened name for linsey-woolsey.

LINSEY-WOOLSEY—A cloth made of linen and wool.

LOG CABIN—*See* pp. 42-46

LOG HOUSE—*See* p. 44

LONG HUNTER—One who spent a season or more in the wilderness on each hunting trip.

MADDER—An herb with a yellow flower, the roots of which were used in making a variety of dyes.

MAGAZINE—A place for keeping gunpowder and other military supplies.

MAUL—A very heavy hammer or mallet. *See* p. 70

NOGGIN—A small mug or cup.

PACK HORSE—A horse used for carrying supplies or goods. *See* p. 14

PADDLE BALL—A game played with paddles and a ball according to handball rules.

PATTEN—A wooden overshoe. *See* p. 102

PEWTER—An alloy principally of tin, with a little antimony, copper and bismuth; inferior kinds have much lead.

PICAYUNE—*See* p. 228

PIETIST—A group of German religious sects which emphasized repentance and faith as an attitude of the heart.

PIGGIN—A small wooden pail with an upright stave for a handle. It was often used as a dipper. *See* p. 186

PINE KNOT—The hard mass formed in a pine tree where a branch grows out. It burns with a bright sputtering flame.

PONE— Bread made of corn meal, with or without milk or eggs.

PORRINGER—A small dish or bowl from which soup, porridge, bread and milk, etc., may be eaten.

POSSET CUP—A two-handled vessel used for making a beverage of hot milk curdled by ale, wine, etc., and often containing spices.

POTATO HOLE—A hole dug several feet deep in the ground in which potatoes or turnips were kept during the winter. The vegetables were covered with loose earth several inches deep to keep the frost away from them.

POTHOOK—An S-shaped hook for hanging pots and kettles over an open fire. *See* p. 46

POWDER HORN—*See* pp. 91 and 122

PUNCHEON—A split log with the flat side smoothed, or a heavy slab.

RAISING BEE—*See* p. 45

RENNET—A lining membrane of the stomach of a calf used for curdling milk in the making of cheese.

RICK—A rounded stack of hay or straw made so that the rain will run off it.

ROSEMARY—A fragrant evergreen shrub whose leaves are used for flavoring and in making perfumes. It is an emblem of remembrance.

RUNLET—Or RUNDLET. A small barrel, usually holding about 18 gallons.

RUSHLIGHT—The dried pith of reeds soaked in grease and burned in tongs or iron clips.

SADDLE-BAG—One of a pair of bags or pouches attached to a saddle, for carrying small articles.

SALTPETER—A salty, white mineral, used in making gunpowder, in preserving meat and also used in medicine.

SANDER—A shaker for sprinkling sand on wet ink in order to dry it.

SAW—A wise saying or a proverb.

SCHNITZEN—*See* p. 110

SCRUB BROOM—*See* p. 48

SCUTCHING KNIFE—*See* p. 76

SCUTCHING TOW—The short fibers produced in separating the woody fibers from the flax.

SET WORK—*See* p. 53

SHOEPACK—*See* p. 55

SILLABUB—Sweetened cream, flavored with wine and beaten to a stiff froth.

SLEEPER—Any of the stones or timbers on or near the ground level supporting the structure above.

SLOP—Any thin, tasteless drink or liquid food

SMALLCLOTHES—Loose fitting knee breeches worn in the 1700's.

SOUTHERNWOOD—A shrub used in beer.

SPELT—*See* p. 124

SPIDER—A cast iron frying pan with a long handle and legs, that can be used over coals on a hearth.

SPIKE BUCK—A male deer in its second year with single-forked antlers.

SPIKENARD—A tall, fragrant plant with greenish flower clusters.

SPIT—A slender pointed rod, usually iron, for holding meat that is being roasted over a fire.

SPLIT BROOM—*See* p. 48

SQUATTER—A person who settles on another's land without right; or a person who settles on public land to acquire ownership of it.

STALK—To approach game cautiously and under cover.

STANCHION—A device which fits loosely about an animal's neck limiting forward and backward motion while permitting lateral motion.

SUTLER—A person who follows an army to sell food, liquor, etc.

Swingle Staff—A wooden instrument like a large knife about two feet long with one thin edge used for beating flax to separate the woody parts from the flax fiber that would be used in weaving.

Tallow Dip—A candle made from the hard fat from sheep, cows, etc., by dipping the wick repeatedly into the liquid tallow. *See* p. 80

Tare and Tret—Teaching how to compute weight and waste, especially in the handling of wool.

Thill—Either of two long pieces of wood between which a horse is hitched to a vehicle; a shaft.

Thong—A narrow strip of leather, used as a fastening—the lash of a whip, a rein, etc.

Three-Cornered Hat—Also called **Three Around**. All players are arranged in a double circle, facing in. The rear players directly behind the front players and 4 ft. back. "It" runs around the outer circle to the right and tags a player. The tagged player immediately tags the one in front of him and running in opposite directions between the two lines the last of the three runners to reach the vacant space is "It".

Tinder—Dry wood shavings or bits of paper that catch fire easily.

Tinder Box—*See* p. 49

Tomahawk—A light ax used by North American Indians as a weapon and a tool. *See* p. 5

Tow—The coarse or broken parts of flax used for tinder and sometimes woven into a coarse cloth for sacking.

Townball—A game much like baseball. A team remains at bat until all the members have been put out. When all but one have retired and this one scores three runs, he may call in to bat any member of his team he chooses.

Trammel—An adjustable pothook for the fireplace crane, from which kettles and pots are suspended over the fire. *See* p. 47

Trencher—A wooden plate or platter.

Trivet—*See* p. 47

TUB MILL—*See* p. 75

TURNIP HOLE—*See* Potato Hole.

TURNOUT—The early name given to a labor strike. *See* p. 229

WEDGE—A piece of wood or metal thick at one end and thin at the other, used in splitting wood or rocks, raising heavy objects, etc.

WEFT—The lengthwise threads of woven material.

WHIPSTOCK—The handle of a whip, usually made from wood.

WHIST—A card game for two pairs of players.

"WONDERS"—A kind of sweet friedcake.

WORM FENCE—A zigzag fence of rails crossing at their ends; also called a snake fence or a rail fence.